Quick Scripture Reference For Life-Issues

Jackson Day

"All Scripture is God-breathed and is useful for teaching, rebuking, correcting and training in righteousness, so that the man of God may be thoroughly equipped for every good work." (2 Timothy 3:16-17 NIV)

Quick Scripture Reference for Life-Issues

©
Jackson Day

Copyright © 2011 by Jackson Day, Opelika, AL. No portion of this book may be reproduced, by any process or technique, without the expressed written consent of the publisher or author.

ISBN 978-0-9797324-5-4

Bible Storytelling Project
http://biblestorytelling.org

OTHER BOOKS BY AUTHOR

- Old Testament Bible Stories ISBN 978-0-9797324-0-9
- New Testament Bible Stories ISBN 978-0-9797324-1-6
- Bible Storytelling Tools ISBN 978-0-9797324-2-3
- Story Crafting ISBN 978-0-9797324-3-0
  The Art of Preparing and Telling Stories
- Outlines of Great Bible Themes ISBN 978-0-9797324-6-1
- Parable Seeds: First Sowing ISBN 978-0-9797324-4-7

TOPIC GUIDE

Preface	1
Addictions: Habits That Enslave a Person	3
Adultery and the Pastor	4
Afflictions and Trials	5
Anger	6
God's Anger	9
Improper Language	10
Bitterness	12
Blame Shifting	13
Borrowing	14
Change to Overcome Sin	15
Confession of Sins	18
Contentment	20
Giving Correction	21
Counsel	23
Covetousness	25
Criticism	26
Curses	27
Death	29
Depression	32
God's Discipline	33
Divorce	34
Drunkenness	36
Envy	37
Fasting	39
Fear	41
Fear of God	43
Forgiveness of Others	45
God's Forgiveness	47
Friendship: Good and Evil	50
Gambling	52
Giving	56
God's Will	58
Habits	59
Homosexuality	60
Honesty	62
Idolatry	64
Becoming like Jesus	66
Laziness	69
Listening	70
Love	72
Lust	74
Lying	75
Marriage	77
Mary, the Mother of Jesus	79
Masturbation	81
Obedience to God's Commandments	82
Discipline by Parents	83

Peace	85
Pedophilia	88
Persecution	89
Pornography	91
Pride	93
Divine Protection from Enemies	95
Quarrels	96
Reacting to Those Who Wrong You	98
Reconciliation	100
Revenge Is Prohibited	101
Self-Opinion	103
Self-Centeredness	104
Self-Control	105
Self-Pity	107
Marriage Sex	109
Sexual Immorality	110
Sickness	113
Silent-Treatment	115
Temptation	116
Thankfulness to God	118
Toxic Parents	120
Violence	123
Work	124
Worry	125
Plan for Dealing with Life-Issues	126

PREFACE

I have been a pastor/missionary for over forty years. I pastored First Baptist Church in Pagosa Springs, Colorado and Walla Walla Baptist Church in Washington. Then, my wife and I were missionaries with the International Mission Board in Brazil for thirty-three years. I was the lead pastor for five church plants. Throughout my ministry, I often did not have a quick answer in counseling situations, or when questions arose when I was visiting. Often I struggled and gave an inadequate answer. So whenever an issue came up that I could not answer, I went home, put a title on a 5X8 note card, searched the Scripture, and made notes of Scripture verses that relate to the issue. My goal was to be prepared the second time an issue was brought up. I carried those cards with me whenever I visited people or when I was counseling. I expanded on those note cards to prepare this book.

This book is compiled to help Christian leaders use the Bible to help people deal with life-issues in their own lives, in counseling, and in answering questions that people are asking. This book is designed to meet the needs of those who use the Bible to understand what God has to say about some of the common issues of life.

I have not listed all the texts that relate to any given issue, only those that I find most helpful. Nor do I use all the listed texts each time I am dealing with an issue. I select the text that I believe most help the person(s) with whom I am talking.

I have included the issues most frequently faced in my ministry; however, I am sure that I have neglected various issues which you and others may face. More than seventy topics are listed. Bible texts and quotations or a summary of the text as it relates to the topics are included. It is my prayer that the accumulations of some notes I made during forty years of ministry will help others who desire to use the Bible to answer their own life-issues and those faced by people who look to them for help.

Scripture texts that are inside of "quotation marks" are taken from the *Holy Bible: New International Version* (NIV). Statements that summarize what the text says about the selected issue are not included inside quotation marks. Statements that are italicized and included inside parenthesis are the author's interpretation or application of the scripture text.

ACKNOWLEDGMENTS

I acknowledge that while living in Brazil for 33 years, I struggled to think and write in Portuguese. As a result, my English suffered. Portuguese is a phonetic language and words are spelled the way they sound. Sometimes I spell an English word phonetically and come up with a word that's not the one I need. Sometimes I use a Portuguese word as though it were an English one.

I acknowledge that I have a writer's blind spot. I see what I think I wrote, instead of what I actually wrote.

I acknowledge the help of two of my friends, Lyn Caudle and Diane Grill. They reviewed this book and provided invaluable counsel and advice.

I acknowledge that I understand why most authors acknowledge the help of their spouses. My wife, Doris Day, helped me with this book more than anyone else. She reviewed the book several times and each time gave me good advice. She has sharp eyes that catch spelling and grammar mistakes. She's stern when correcting my writing mistakes, but she's gentle when correcting my other mistakes.

ADDICTIONS: HABITS THAT ENSLAVE A PERSON

Rom 6:6	We were crucified with Jesus so that we should no longer be slaves to sin.
Rom 6:16-22	A person is a slave to the one he obeys, whether to sin or obedience (16). Those who used to be slaves to sin have been set free from sin by obeying the teaching to which they were entrusted (17-18). The one who offered the parts of his body in slavery to impurity can now offer them in slavery to righteousness (19). There are benefits to being set free from sin (22).
Rom 7:25	Paul experienced an internal conflict: in his mind he was a slave to God's law, but in the sinful nature he was a slave to the law of sin.
1 Cor 6:9-12	Addictive behavior is typical of those who will not inherit the Kingdom of God. Some had been addicted, but were washed, sanctified, justified in the name of Jesus and by the Spirit.
Gal 4:8	Those who do not know God are slaves to those who are not gods.
Gal 5:1	Christ set us free; do not again become burdened by a yoke of slavery.
Eph 5:18	Do not be drunk on wine; instead, be filled with the Spirit.
Tit 3:3-6	Christ saves one from slavery to passions and pleasure.
2 Pet 2:19	A person is a slave to whatever has mastered him.
Rev 21:8; 22:15	Addictive behavior is typical of those who will be in hell.

ADULTERY AND THE PASTOR

Jer 23:13-14	Prophets who commit adultery, and live a lie, lead God's people astray and are guilty of horrible things. They strengthen the hands of evildoers.
Jer 29:20-23	It is an outrageous thing for a prophet to commit adultery and speak lies in God's name (23). Such will be cursed (21-22).
1 Cor 6:12-19	Flee from adultery; it is a sin against one's own body.
2 Tim 2:22	Paul advised the young pastor, Timothy, to flee the desires of youth.
2 Tim 3:5-9	Have nothing to do with those who have a form of godliness but deny its power (5). They gain control over weak-willed women and are swayed by all kinds of evil desire (6). Such men oppose the truth and are rejected by the faith (8).
2 Tim 3:13	"Evil men and impostors will go from bad to worse, deceiving and being deceived."
2 Pet 2:2-19	False teachers and prophets will follow shameful ways and bring the way of truth into disrepute (2). Their pleasure is to carouse in broad daylight (13). With eyes full of adultery, they never stop sinning; they seduce the unstable (14). They left the straight way (15). Such men are springs without water (17). They promise freedom while they themselves are slaves of depravity (19).
1 Tim 5:19-20	Do not accept an accusation against an elder unless it is brought by two or three witnesses. Publicly rebuke those who sin.

AFFLICTIONS AND TRIALS

1 Pet 1:6-7	You may have to suffer grief in all kinds of trials so that your faith may be proved genuine and may result in praise, glory and honor when Jesus Christ is revealed.
Jam 1:2-4	Trials develop patience in us.
Deut 8:2-5	God disciplines just as a parent disciplines his child.
Heb 12:5-11	God disciplines his children whom he loves (5-6). Discipline is painful but produces benefits (11).
Rev 3:19-20	Jesus rebukes and disciplines those he loves.
Rom 8:28	In everything, God works for the good of those who love him.
1 Cor 10:13	God will never give a person more than he can bear.
Examples of People Who Suffered Afflictions	
Job 1:1-22	Job, a godly man, was severely tried by the devil. He lost his possessions, his children, and his health.
Psa 119:67-68, 71-72, 75-76	The psalmist's affections taught him to obey God's words.
Isa 38:15-19	King Hezekiah praised God for the benefits that came as a result of the anguish of his soul.
Jn 9:1-3	The man blind from birth was not made blind as a result of sins, but so that the work of God might be displayed in his life.
2 Cor 12:7-10	Paul was given a thorn in the flesh that tormented him. God refused to remove it but gave him sufficient grace and made him strong in his weakness.

ANGER

Examples of People Becoming Angry

Gen 4:5-8	Cain became angry and killed his brother Abel.
1 Sam 18:8-11	Saul's anger against David made him jealous and provoked him to attempt murder.
2 Kg 5:8-12	Naaman's anger at the way the prophet Elisha treated him almost prevented him from receiving a cure from God.
2 Chr 16:7-10	King Asa served the Lord for 36 years of his kingship. When he made a treaty with an evil king, the prophet Hanani confronted Asa because he relied on a king and not on the Lord God. Asa became angry, put the prophet in prison and began to brutally oppress some of the people.
Est 3:5-6	The noble Haman became angry when Mordecai the Jew would not kneel before him. He plotted to kill Mordecai and all the Jews.
Dan 3:19	Nebuchadnezzar was furious with the three Jewish men who refused to bow down to the golden image. He had them thrown into the furnace.
Lk 4:28	The people of Nazareth became angry at Jesus' words and tried to kill him.
Ac 19:27-28	Demetrius provoked a mob in Ephesus to riot with the accusation that Paul had dishonored the goddess Artemis and her temple.

Warnings Against Anger

Prov 14:17, 29	The angry person does foolish things.
Prov 15:1	"A harsh word stirs up anger."
Prov 15:18	The hot-tempered person stirs up dissension.
Prov 19:19	A hot-tempered person must pay the penalty. He needs to be rescued again and again.
Prov 25:28	A person who lacks self-control is like a city without protection.
Prov 29:8	"Wise men turn away anger."
Prov 29:11	A fool gives vent to his anger; a wise person has self-control.

Prov 29:22	An angry person stirs up dissensions and commits many sins.
Prov 30:33	"Stirring up anger produces strife."
Mat 5:22	Anyone who is angry with his brother will be subject to God's judgment.
1 Cor 13:5	Love is not easily angered.
Advice to the Angry Person	
Gen 4:5-7	Anger is compared to a wild animal crouching at the door, ready to pounce on the angry person. The angry person must tame it.
Psa 4:4	"In your anger, do not sin."
Psa 37:8	Refrain from anger; forsake wrath.
Prov 16:32	"Better...a man who controls his temper than one who takes a city."
Prov 19:11	It is to a person's glory to overlook an offense.
Prov 20:22; 24:29	When wronged, do not seek revenge.
Prov 21:14	"A gift given in secret soothes anger."
Prov 22:24	Do not associate with a person who is easily angered.
Ecc 7:9	Do not be quickly provoked. Anger resides in the lap of fools.
Mat 5:39	Do not seek revenge, accept mistreatment.
Eph 4:26, 29, 31-32	When angry, do not sin. Resolve the anger before the next day. Do not allow anger to produce unwholesome talk (29), bitterness, rage, brawling, slander or malice (31). Get rid of rage and anger (31).
Col 3:8	Rid yourself of anger and rage.
Gal 5:19-21	Fits of rage belong to the sinful nature.
Gal 5:22-25	Part of the fruit of the Spirit is self-control (22). Those who belong to Christ Jesus have crucified the sinful nature with its passions. This includes fits of rage (24).
Jam 1:19-20	Everyone should be slow to speak and slow to anger. Anger does not bring about the righteous life that God desires.

Righteous Anger	
Ex 32:19	Moses' anger burned when he saw the golden calf in the Israelites' camp.
Lev 10:16	Moses became angry with the priest who did not follow instructions with the sin offering.
Nu 16:15	Moses became angry at a group that opposed him and Aaron (3).
1 Sam 11:6	Saul became angry when he heard that the Ammonites planned to put out the right eye of all the men of Jabesh.
Neh 5:6	Nehemiah became angry at the nobles who were exploiting the poor.
Mk 10:14	Jesus became indignant at the disciples who prevented the children from coming to him.

Anger becomes sin when expressed by either exploding or holding it inside and letting it burn slowly.

Anger correctly expressed is against the problem. Direct the energy generated by anger against the problem.

Anger wrongly expressed is against a person: whether against another person or against oneself.

The angry person seeks to hurt another; however, he also hurts himself.

GOD'S ANGER

Ex 4:14	God's anger burned against Moses when he kept refusing to return to Egypt.
Ex 22:24	God's anger is aroused when people take advantage of widows or orphans.
Ex 34:6; Psa 86:15; 193:8	The Lord is slow to anger, but abounding in love.
Num 11:1, 10	The Lord became angry at the Israelites who complained about their hardships.
Num 22:22	The Lord was angry with Balaam when he was on his way to curse God's people.
Num 25:3	The Lord was angry with the Israelites who joined in worshiping Baal.
Deut 4:25	Becoming corrupt and making idols provoke God to anger.
Psa 106:29, 32, 40	When wandering in the wilderness, the Israelites provoked God to anger by their wicked deeds.
Jos 22:18	If you rebel against the Lord, he will become angry.
1 Ki 11:9	God became angry with Solomon.
Mk 3:5	Jesus was angry at the legalistic, traditional-bound Pharisees.
Mk 10:13-16	Jesus became angry when the disciples rebuked parents who were bringing little children to Jesus (14).

IMPROPER LANGUAGE

Power of Words

Prov 10:19	When words are many, sin is present; he who holds his tongue is wise.
Prov 18:21	"The tongue has the power of life and death."
Jam 3:2	If anyone is never at fault in what he says, he is perfect.

Slander/False Testimony

Ex 20:16	Do not give false testimony against your neighbor.
Ex 23:1	"Do not spread false reports."
Eph 4:31; Col 3:8-9	Rid yourselves of slander.
Tit 3:2	Slander no one; be peaceable and considerate.
Jam 4:11	Do not slander one another. "Anyone who speaks against his brother or judges him speaks against the law and judges it."

Lying

Psa 10:7; 58:3	The wicked arrogant person's mouth is full of lies and threats.
Prov 6:17-19	The Lord hates a lying tongue and a false witness who lies.
Prov 26:24-26	"A malicious man disguises himself with his lips, but in his heart he harbors deceit....His malice may be concealed by deception, but his wickedness will be exposed."
Eph 4:25, 31	"Put off falsehood and speak truthfully" (25). "Get rid of...slander" (31).
Col 3:8-9	"Do not lie to each other."

Harsh Words

Prov 15:1	"A gentle answer turns away wrath, but a harsh word stirs up anger."
Prov 29:11	"A fool gives full vent to his anger."

Arguing

Eph 4:31	"Get rid of...brawling."

2 Tim 2:23-24	Have nothing to do with stupid, senseless controversies; the Lord's servant must not be quarrelsome.
Tit 3:2	Slander no one; be peaceable and considerate.
Filthy Language	
Psa 109:17-19	Curses rest on those who love to pronounce curses.
Jam 3:9-12	Praises and cursing should not come out of the same mouth.
Eph 4:29	"Do not let unwholesome talk come out of your mouths, but only what is helpful for building others up according to their needs."
Col 3:8-9	Rid yourselves of filthy language.

Improper Language is related to: Addictions, Habits that Enslave a Person, Change to Overcome Sin, and Curses.

BITTERNESS

Warnings Against Bitterness

Lev 19:17	"Do not hate your brother in your heart."
Prov 17:25	A foolish child brings bitterness to his parents.
Prov 26:24-26	"A malicious man disguises himself with his lips, but in his heart he harbors deceit....His malice may be concealed by deception, but his wickedness will be exposed."
Gal 5:15	Those who keep on biting and devouring each other will be destroyed by each other.
Gal 5:19	"Fits of rage" are included in the acts of the sinful nature.
Eph 4:31	"Get rid of all bitterness, rage and anger...along with every form of malice."
Col 3:21	"Fathers, do not embitter your children."
Heb 12:15	See to it that no bitter root grows up to cause trouble and defile many.
Jam 3:14	The person with bitter envy does not have wisdom from God.

Examples of Bitterness

Ruth 1:13, 20	Naomi was bitter over her circumstances in life.
1 Sam 1:10	Hannah felt bitter because she had no children.
2 Kg 4:27	The Shunammite woman was in bitter distress after her only son died.
Job 3:20; 7:11; 10:1; 27:2	Job was bitter of soul.
Psa 73:21-22	When the psalmist's spirit was embittered, he was senseless, ignorant and acted like a brute beast before God.
Ac 8:23	The Samaritan Simon was full of bitterness.

BLAME SHIFTING

Gen 3:12-13	After eating the forbidden fruit: Adam shifted the blame to God and the woman; Eve shifted the blame to the snake.
Gen 4:8-13	Cain did not assume responsibility for killing his brother.
Ex 32:22-24	After Aaron made the golden calf, he blamed the people.
1 Sam 13:12	King Saul offered excuses to justify his wrongdoing for usurping the functions of the priest and offering the burnt offering.
1 Sam 15:21	King Saul shifted the blame from himself to his soldiers for keeping the forbidden spoils of war.
1 Kg 18:17-18	King Ahab accused prophet Elijah of being a troublemaker and did not assume responsibility for the consequences of his own sins.
Prov 19:3	"A man's own folly ruins his life, yet his heart rages against the Lord." *(People often blame God for problems that are the results of their own sins.)*
Rom 1:20	People are without excuse for their sins.

Blame Shifting is related to: Change to Overcome Sin, Confession of Sins.

BORROWING

Ex 22:14	If a person borrows an animal from his neighbor and it is injured while the owner is not present, the borrower must make restitution.
Deut 15:6; 28:12	It is a blessing for a people to be able to lend without needing to borrow.
Psa 37:21	"The wicked borrow and do not repay."
Psa 37:21,26	The righteous are generous and lend freely.
Psa 112:5	Good will come to him who lends freely.
Prov 22:7	"The borrower is servant to the lender."
Mat 5:42	"Do not turn away from the one who wants to borrow from you."
Lk 6:34-36	In the context of speaking about love for one's enemies, Jesus taught that his followers should lend without expecting anything back. Then they will be like God the Father who is kind to the ungrateful and wicked.
2 Thes 3:10	The person who will not work shall not eat.

CHANGE TO OVERCOME SIN

God Enables a Person to Change

Ezek 36:25-27	God gives us a new heart and a new spirit (26). God removes our heart of stone and gives us a heart of flesh (26). God puts his Spirit in us and moves us to follow his decrees and obey his Laws (27).
Jn 8:32-36	"The truth will set you free" (32). "Everyone who sins is a slave to sin" (34). "If the Son sets you free, you will be free indeed" (36).
Rom 6:18	"You have been set free from sin and have become slaves to righteousness."
Rom 8:2	Paul stated that the law of the Spirit of life in Christ Jesus made him free from the law of sin and death.
Rom 8:9-11	If Christ is in a person, that person's body is dead because of sin, yet his spirit is alive because of righteousness. The Spirit who raised Jesus from the dead will also give life to his mortal body through his Spirit, who lives in him.
1 Cor 6:9-11	The sexually immoral, idolaters, adulterers, prostitutes, homosexuals, thieves, greedy, drunkards, slanderers, swindlers, etc. can overcome sin by God's power and grace when they are justified in the name of the Lord Jesus Christ and by the Spirit of God.
2 Cor 3:18	"We...are being transformed into his likeness with ever-increasing glory, which comes from the Lord, who is the Spirit."
2 Cor 5:17	"If anyone is in Christ, he is a new creation; the old has gone, the new has come!"
2 Cor 9:8	"God is able to make all grace abound to you, so that in all things at all times, having all that you need, you will abound in every good work."
Php 2:12-13	"Continue to work out your salvation with fear and trembling, for it is God who works in you to will and to act according to his good purpose."
2 Pet 1:3	"His divine power has given us everything we need for life and godliness through our knowledge of him who called us by his own glory and goodness."

1 Jn 3:9	"No one who is born of God will continue to sin, because God's seed remains in him; he cannot go on sinning, because he has been born of God."
Each Person Has Responsibility to Change	
Rom 6:10-23	"Count yourselves dead to sin but alive to God in Christ Jesus" (11). "Do not let sin reign in your mortal body" (12). "Do not offer the parts of your body to sin, as instruments of wickedness, but rather offer yourselves to God...and offer the parts of your body to him as instruments of righteousness" (13). "Just as you used to offer the parts of your body in slavery to impurity...so now offer them in slavery to righteousness leading to holiness" (19).
Rom 8:13-14	"If you live according to the sinful nature, you will die; but if by the Spirit you put to death the misdeeds of the body, you will live, because those who are led by the Spirit of God are sons of God."
Rom 12:1-3	Offer your bodies as living sacrifices (1). Do not conform to the pattern of this world, but be transformed by the renewing of your mind (2). Do not think of yourself more highly than you ought (3).
Eph 4:17-32	You must not live as the Gentiles do, in the futility of their thinking (17). Put off your old self, which is being corrupted by its deceitful desires (22). Be renewed in the spirit of your mind (23). Put on the new self, created to be like God in true righteousness and holiness (24). There is a list of actions and attitudes that are to be taken off and those that are to be put on in their place (25-32).
Php 3:12-14	Press on to take hold of that for which Christ Jesus took hold of us. Forget what is behind and strain toward what is ahead. Press on toward the goal to win the prize for which God has called us.
Col 3:1-17	If you have been risen with Christ, seek those things which are above (1). Put to death whatever belongs to your earthly nature. A list is given of characteristics that are to be put to death (5-6). A list is given of characteristics that we have an obligation to rid ourselves of (8-10). A list is given of characteristics that we have an obligation to clothe ourselves with (12-17).

1 Tim 4:7	"Train yourself to be godly."
Heb 12:1	"Let us throw off everything that hinders and the sin that so easily entangles and let us run with perseverance the race marked out for us."
Jam 4:7	"Submit yourselves then to God. Resist the devil and he will flee from you."
2 Pet 3:14	Make every effort to be found spotless, blameless and at peace with the Lord.
Help for Overcoming Sin	
Psa 51:10	The psalmist prayed for God to create in him a clean heart.
2 Tim 3:16-17	"All Scripture...is useful for teaching, rebuking, correcting and training in righteousness, so that the man of God may be thoroughly equipped for every good work."
Examples of People Who Changed	
Mat 26:74; Ac 4:8-20	Peter, the cowardly-cursing fisherman, became a man who spoke about Jesus with courage.
Mk 5:5; 5:15	The uncontrollable demoniac man became a quiet disciple.
Lk 9:53-54; 1 Jn 4:7	John the vindictive Jew became the apostle of love.
Lk 15:24	In the parable of the Prodigal Son, the son who had been dead to his father returned alive to his father.
Jn 4:17-18, 29	The immoral Samaritan woman became an evangel of truth.
Ac 9:1; 21:13	Saul the bloodthirsty persecutor of Christians became Paul the tenderhearted brother in Christ.
Ac 16:24; 16:33	The cruel Philippian jailer became a sympathetic friend to his prisoners.

Change to Overcome Sin is related to: Confession of Sins, and Becoming Like Jesus.

CONFESSION OF SINS

Lev 5:5	The one who is guilty must confess how he has sinned.
Num 5:7	The one who wronged another must both confess his sins and make restitution.
1 Kg 8:33-35	People who are suffering divine punishment, as a result of their sins, must confess their sins and turn from their wicked ways.
Ezr 10:1	Ezra confessed the sins of his forefathers and nation.
Ezr 10:11	Ezra called on the people to confess their sins to God and to do his will.
Neh 1:6	Nehemiah confessed the sins of himself, his ancestors and his nation.
Neh 9:2-3	The Israelites confessed their sins and the wickedness of their ancestors.
Psa 32:5	David confessed his iniquities and God forgave him.
Prov 28:13	"He who conceals his sins does not prosper; but whoever confesses and renounces them finds mercy."
Dan 9:20	Daniel was praying, speaking to God, and confessing his sins and the sins of his people.
Lk 15:18-21	The prodigal son confessed he had sinned against God and against his father.
Mat 3:6	The people went out to John the Baptist, confessed their sins and were baptized.
Mat 3:8	The one who confesses his sins should produce fruit in keeping with repentance.
Ac 19:18-19	In Ephesus, many who believed in Jesus openly confessed their evil deeds, and they burned their books related to the practice of sorcery.

Jam 5:16	When praying for the sick, confess your sins and pray for each other.
1 Jn 1:9	"If we confess our sins, he is faithful and just and will forgive us our sins and purify us from all unrighteousness."

Observations:
1. The one who has sinned should confess his sins both to God and to those who were wronged, and he should do all within his power to make restitution.
2. Sins that were committed in public should be confessed publicly. Also, sins that are public knowledge should be confessed publicly.
3. Sins that remain hidden from the public need only be confessed to those who were harmed by the sin.
4. In rare situations, if confession of sins to others would complicate the lives of the ones who heard the confession instead of bringing healing, discernment may require that confession be made only to God.

CONTENTMENT

1 Tim 6:6-10	"Godliness with contentment is great gain" (6). "The love of money is a root of all kinds of evil" (10).
Heb 13:5	Keep your lives free from the love of money and be content with what you have, because God will never leave nor forsake you.
Php 4:11-13	Paul learned the secret of being content in any and every situation.
Lk 12:15	"Be on your guard against all kinds of greed; a man's life does not consist in the abundance of his possessions."
Mk 4:1-20	In the Parable of the Sower, the seed that fell among the thorns (7) teaches that the worries of this life, the deceitfulness of wealth and the desires for other things choke God's word, making it unfruitful (18-20).
Prov 15:16-17	"Better a little with the fear of the Lord than great wealth with turmoil. Better a meal of vegetables where there is love than a fattened calf with hatred."
Prov 17:1	"Better a dry crust with peace and quiet than a house full of feasting with strife."
Prov 23:4-5	Do not wear yourself out to get rich. Show restraint; riches will sprout wings and fly off.
Prov 30:8-9	"Give me neither poverty not riches, but give me only my daily bread. Otherwise, I may have too much and disown you and say, 'Who is the Lord?' Or I may become poor and steal and so dishonor the name of my God."

GIVING CORRECTION

Prov 9:7	"Whoever corrects a mocker, invites insults."
Psa 19:11	The Word of the Lord warns the servant of the Lord.
Eze 3:17-21	God's spokesman is a watchman with an obligation to warn those who do evil.
Mat 18:15-18	Jesus gives the procedure for church discipline: If your brother sins against you, go and show him his fault. If he will not listen, take one or two others along. If he refuses to listen to them, tell it to the church; if he refuses to listen to the church, treat him as you would a pagan.
Col 3:16	"Let the word of Christ dwell in you richly as you teach and admonish one another."
Gal 6:1	Restore the one caught in a sin gently. While correcting another, be cautious or you will be tempted.
1 Thes 5:14	An obligation, "Warn those who are idle, encourage the timid, help the weak, be patient with everyone."
2 Thes 3:14-15	When correcting a fellow Christian, do not treat him as an enemy, but warn him as a brother. Do not associate with the person who does not obey biblical instruction.
1 Tim 5:19-22	Instruction for correcting a pastor/elder. An accusation must be brought by two or three witnesses (19). Those who sin are to be rebuked publicly (20). These instructions are to be followed without partiality or favoritism (21).
2 Tim 2:14	The spiritual leader should keep reminding and warning others about inappropriate behavior.
2 Tim 4:2	A pastor should correct, rebuke and encourage with patience and careful instruction.
Tit 3:10	"Warn a divisive person once, and then warn him a second time. After that, have nothing to do with him."

Jam 5:19-20	"Whoever turns a sinner from the error of his way will save him from death and cover over a multitude of sins" (20).
Rev 2:14-16	Jesus rebukes the church that does not correct and discipline those who teach false doctrine.

COUNSEL

Listen to Counsel

Psa 119:24	God's Word should serve as a counselor.
Prov 10:17	"He who heeds discipline shows the way to life, but whoever ignores correction leads others astray."
Prov 12:15	"The way of a fool seems right to him, but a wise man listens to advice."
Prov 13:10	Wisdom is found in those who take advice.
Prov 27:29	Friends give earnest counsel.

Need for Counsel

Prov 11:14	"For lack of guidance a nation falls, but many advisers make victory sure."
Prov 15:22	"Plans fail for lack of counsel, but with many advisers they succeed."
Prov 19:20	Listen to advice and you will be wise.
Prov 20:18	Make plans by seeking advice.
Prov 24:6	"For waging war you need guidance, and for victory many advisers."

Evil Counsel

Psa 1:1	"Blessed is the person who does not walk in the counsel of the wicked."
Prov 12:5	"The advice of the wicked is deceitful."
Isa 19:11	Counselors of the wicked give senseless advice.
Eze 11:12	Those plotting evil give wicked advice.

Those Who Refuse Counsel

2 Chr 25:16	God destroys those who refuse to listen to his counsel.
2 Chr 36:16	Those who despise counsel given by God's messengers will experience God's wrath, against which there is no remedy.
Prov 1:25, 30	The person who rejects wise advice will experience calamity.
Prov 5:12-14	The person who refuses to listen to counsel (7) at the end of his life will cry out in despair.

Quick Scripture Reference for Life-Issues © Jackson Day

Prov 12:15	"The way of a fool seems right to him, but a wise man listens to advice."
When to Refuse to Give Counsel	
Prov 9:7-9	"Do not rebuke a mocker or he will hate you."
The Holy Spirit Is a Counselor	
Jn 14:16, 26; 15:26; 16:7	The Holy Spirit is God's counselor sent to the followers of Jesus.
Examples of Accepting or Rejecting Counsel	
Ex 18:19	Moses acted on advice he received from his father-in-law.
Psa 32:8	After David confessed his sins, he offered counsel to others.
1 Kg 12:6-14	King Rehoboam listened to the wrong advice and lost the support of 10 of the 12 tribes.
1 Kg 12:28	King Jeroboam listened to the wrong advice and led Israel into idolatry.

COVETOUSNESS

Ex 20:17	You shall not covet.
Prov 23:4-5	Do not wear yourself out to get rich. Show restraint; riches will sprout wings and fly off.
Mat 6:19-21	Do not store up for yourselves treasures on earth; store up for yourselves treasures in heaven. For where your treasure is, there your heart will be also.
Lk 9:46-48	Jesus corrected the disciples who were arguing among themselves as to which of them would be the greatest.
Col 3:5	Put greed to death.

CRITICISM

Mat 7:1; Rm 2:1	Danger: the one who passes critical judgment on others is condemning himself.
Mat 7:3-5	A person should correct his own faults in order to be qualified to correct the faults of others.
Rom 14:1-22	Do not judge and condemn others on disputable matters (1-8). Stop passing judgment on others. Avoid putting any stumbling block in your brother's way (13).
1 Tim 6:4	An interest in controversies and quarrels about words result in envy, strife, malicious talk, evil suspicions, and constant friction.
Gal 6:1	If someone is caught in a sin, restore him gently; watch or you also will be tempted.

CURSES

Divine Curses

Gen 3:17	After eating the forbidden fruit, Adam came under a divine curse.
Gen 4:11	After killing his brother, Cain came under a divine curse.
Deut 11:26-28	The choices a person makes determine if he will receive a divine curse or a divine blessing. The one who obeys God's commands receives a blessing; the one who disobeys God's commands receives a curse.
Deut 27:15-26	The text lists actions which place a person under a divine curse: idolatry; dishonoring father or mother; changing property boundary; leading the blind astray; withholding justice from unprotected people; having sex with a parent's spouse; having sex with an animal; committing incest; secretly murdering; murdering for money; disobeying God's Law.
Psa 109:17-19	Curses rest on those who love to pronounce curses.
Jer 11:3	Jews who disobey the terms of the covenant that God established with their ancestors are cursed.
Gal 3:10	The person who does not rely on faith, but instead relies on himself obeying God's Law is under a curse.
2 Pet 2:14	Religious leaders who follow the corrupt desire of the sinful nature (10), who commit adultery (14) and deceive for money (15) are cursed (14).

Pronouncing Curses Is Prohibited

Rom 12:14	The Christian should bless, instead of cursing, those who persecute him.
Jam 3:9-10	Curses should not come out of the mouths of those who praise the Lord.

People Who Pronounce Curses

Ex 21:17; Prov 20:20; 30:11	Anyone who curses his father or mother deserves punishment.

Psa 109:17-19	Curses rest on those who love to pronounce curses.
Psa 10:7; 59:12	The mouth of the wicked and arrogant is full of curses, lies and threats.
Protection from Curses	
Prov 26:2	A curse does not rest on a person who does not deserve it. Rather, the undeserved curse is like a bird that flies without direction.
Gal 3:13	"Christ redeemed us from the curse of the Law by becoming a curse for us."
Rev 22:3	There will be no curse in Heaven's new city.

DEATH

All Will Die

Psa 49:10	Wise men die; likewise, the fool and the senseless person perish.
Ecc 8:8	No person has power to retain the spirit; neither has he power over the day of his death.
Rom 5:12	Death comes to all men.
Heb 9:27	A person is destined to die once. After death he is destined to face judgment.

Death Has Been Conquered

1 Cor 15:26	"The last enemy to be destroyed is death."
1 Cor 15:50-57	"Death has been swallowed up in victory" (54). "The sting of death is sin, and the power of sin is the law. But thanks be to God! He gives us the victory through our Lord Jesus Christ" (56-57).
2 Tim 1:10	Our Savior Jesus Christ has destroyed death.
Rev 21:1-4	In the new heaven and the new earth, there will be no more death or mourning or crying. The old order of things has passed away.

Comfort for Those Who Grieve the Death of a Loved One

2 Sam 12:18-23	After David's infant son died, he was comforted by the fact that one day he would go to him (23).
Psa 23:1-6	"Even though I walk through the valley of the shadow of death, I will fear no evil" (4).
Rom 8:38-39	Nothing, not even death, can separate us from the love of God.
1 Thes 4:13-18	The believer in Jesus should not grieve at the death of a brother in Christ like those who have no hope (13). When the Lord comes down from heaven, the dead in Christ will rise first (16).

Death of the Wicked

Psa 37:36	The wicked and ruthless person, who had flourished like a green tree in its native soil, passed away and was no more.

Ecc 8:8	"No one has power over the day of his death....As no one is discharged in time of war, so wickedness will not release those who practice it."
Eze 18:23	God does not take pleasure in the death of the wicked; rather, he is pleased when they turn from their ways and live.
Lk 12:20	In the parable of the *Rich Fool*, God told the man who stored up great wealth for himself, "You fool! This very night your life will be demanded from you."
Lk 16:19-31	In the parable of the *Rich Man and Lazarus*, the rich man died and went to hell (22), a place of torment (23).
Death of the Righteous	
Prov 14:34	The righteous has hope in his death.
Psa 116:15	"Precious in the sight of the Lord is the death of his saints."
Lk 16:22	In Jesus' parable, when the beggar died, he was carried by the angels into Abraham's bosom.
Assurances for the Christian Who Faces Death	
Psa 23:1-6	Even though I walk through the valley of the shadow of death, I will fear no evil, for you are with me; your rod and your staff they comfort me (4). I will dwell in the house of the Lord forever (6).
Jn 10:14-15	Jesus gives his sheep eternal life. No one can snatch them out of his hand.
Jn 11:17-26	After the death of Lazarus, Jesus told Martha, "Your brother will rise again....I am the resurrection and the life. He who believes in me will live, even though he dies; and whoever lives and believes in me will never die" (23-26).
Jn 14:1-4	In the Father's house there are many rooms. Jesus has gone there to prepare a place for his followers.
Rom 8:38-39	Nothing, not even death, can separate us from the love of God.
Rom 14:8	"If we live, we live to the Lord; if we die, we die to the Lord. So whether we live or die, we belong to the Lord."

Php 1:20-25	Paul said, "For to me, to live is Christ and to die is gain" (21).
Rev 14:13	"Blessed are the dead who die in the Lord from now on....they will rest from their labor, for their deeds will follow them."

DEPRESSION

Gen 4:6-7	Depression results in sin crouching at your door. It desires to have you, but you must master it. Cain's depression was due to guilt.
1 Kg 19:1-18	The depressed person should both take care of his body and act to assume responsibility. When Elijah was depressed, God let him sleep (5), provided him with food (6), and gave him the responsibility to anoint two kings and a prophet (15-16).
Psa 32:3-4	Unconfessed sins provoke depression.
Psa 39:2	Silence, that is the result of refusing to talk, provokes depression.
Prov 18:14	Who can support a crushed spirit?
2 Cor 4:8-18	Don't be distressed by tribulations. There is a positive side for every distressed situation (8-9). The one who raised the Lord Jesus from the dead will also raise us (14). Do not lose heart (16). Our momentary troubles are achieving for us an eternal glory (17-18).

Depression is related to: Anger, Bitterness, Self-Pity, Thankfulness to God, Worry, and Change to Overcome Sin.

GOD'S DISCIPLINE

Prov 3:11-12	Do not resent the Lord's discipline or rebuke (11). The Lord disciplines those he loves (12).
Jn 15:2	The Father cuts off every branch that bears no fruit; he prunes every branch that bears fruit so that it will be even more fruitful.
1 Cor 11:29-34	Everyone who eats and drinks the Lord's Supper without recognizing the body of the Lord, eats and drinks judgment on himself (29). God disciplines with sickness and death (30-31). He disciplines Christians so they will not be condemned with the world (32).
Heb 12:10-11	"God disciplines us for our good, that we may share in his holiness. No discipline seems pleasant at the time, but painful. Later on, however, it produces a harvest of righteousness and peace for those who have been trained by it."
1 Pet 4:13	"Rejoice that you participate in the sufferings of Christ."

DIVORCE

Gen 2:24	A person should leave his parents, be united to his spouse and they will become one flesh.
Deut 24:1-4	Divorce was permitted by the law and finalized with a certificate of divorce. The divorced person could marry another. After a second marriage, it was not permitted to return to the first marriage partner.
Mal 2:14-16	God hates divorce.
Mat 2:18-19	Joseph was called a righteous man when he was preparing to divorce pregnant Mary, and Joseph knew he couldn't be the father.
Mat 5:31-32	Divorce was prohibited by Jesus, except in the case of marital unfaithfulness (*illicit sexual activity*).
Mat 19:3-8 // Mk 10:3-9	People should not separate what God has joined together. Divorce is not God's intention; however, it is permitted because of the hardness of people's hearts. Divorce is prohibited, except for marital unfaithfulness.
Mat 19:9	The person who divorces a faithful marriage partner in order to marry another is guilty of adultery.
Rom 7:1-3	A husband and wife are bound together until death separates them.
1 Cor 7:10-25 Rom 7:2; 12:18	A believer should not separate from his spouse (10). If one separates, he must remain unmarried or else be reconciled (11). The person who is abandoned by a spouse is no longer bound by the marriage. If an unbelieving spouse wants to depart, he may do so (15). *(See Rom 7:2. The spouse is released from the law of marriage.)* God called us to live in peace (1 Cor 7:15; Rom 12:18).
1 Cor 7:15	God called us to live in peace. *(This would allow a Christian to separate from a toxic spouse who is the source of constant conflict.)*
1 Cor 7:15	The non-Christian spouse has the right to seek divorce from a Christian; the Christian does not have that right.
1 Cor 7:39-40	The Christian should only marry a person who belongs to the Lord.

It takes two people to marry, but only one person to divorce. God hates divorce; however, God does not hate divorced people.

Jesus and the apostle Paul upheld the right to "just-cause" divorce and remarriage. Christians have the right to divorce and remarriage in the case of:
- Marital unfaithfulness (*sexual sin of any kind--adultery, homosexuality; incest, pornography, etc.*).
- Abandonment. *(Abandonment is not restricted to physical relocation. It can also include emotional distance created by an addiction to drugs, alcohol, pornography or abuse.)*
- Impossibility of peace. God called us to live in peace. God plans for a Christian to live in a moral environment within the framework of a peaceful relationship. (*It is my interpretation that a Christian is not required to live within a relationship that is outside the morality of Bible teaching. If the spouse is a murderer, thief, liar, slanderer, or abusive, hostile, violent, or guilty of criminal or immoral behavior, the Christian is not required to stay in the relationship merely because that spouse has not committed sexual sins against the spouse.*)

A Christian seeking divorce with "just-cause" can be right with God.

The Christian who divorces without "just-cause" should seek to be reconciled or remain single. Without a "just-cause" for divorcing, there is no just-cause to remarry without being guilty of the sin of adultery against the former spouse.

The person who divorced without "just-cause" and then remarried, needs to confess his sins to God and the wronged spouse. Sins that are confessed are forgiven by God (1 Jn 1:9). Then he needs to work on obeying God to make the new marriage work.

DRUNKENNESS

Prov 20:1	"Wine is a mocker and beer a brawler; whoever is led astray by them is not wise."
Prov 23:20-21	Do not join those who drink too much wine, for drunkards become poor.
Prov 23:29-35	The text describes the calamities that await those who linger over wine.
Prov 31:4-6	When those in leadership drink wine and beer, they forget what the law decrees and deprive the oppressed of their rights.
Isa 28:1-4	One of the reasons that God's wrath was upon Israel was its sin of drunkenness.
Isa 28:7-8	Isaiah describes a picture of spiritual leaders becoming drunk and losing their moral judgment.
Lk 21:34	Jesus warns to be careful and don't become drunk or hung over.
1 Cor 5:11	The Christian should not associate with anyone who calls himself a Christian, yet is a drunkard.
1 Cor 6:9-11	The apostle Paul says that no drunkard shall enter the Kingdom of God (9-10); however, a person can be saved from drunkenness and set free (11).
Eph 5:18	"Do not get drunk on wine, which leads to debauchery; instead, be filled with the Spirit."
1 Pet 4:3	The Christian should not live in drunkenness like the pagans choose to do.
Examples of Drunkenness	
Gen 9:20-22	Noah lost his composure and exposed himself.
Gen 19:32-35	Lot lost consciousness and committed incest.
2 Sam 13:28-29	The influence of alcohol had a part in the death of Amnom. In his drunken condition, he could not resist when attacked.
Dan 5:1-30	King Belshazzar lost his sobriety, his kingdom and his life.

Drunkenness is related to: Addictions, Lying, and Change to Overcome Sin.

ENVY

An Action of the Sinful Nature

Mk 7:22	Envy comes from inside a person and makes him unclean.
Rom 1:29	Godless and wicked people (1:13) are full of envy (1:29).
Rom 13:13	Jealousy is an indecent behavior.
1 Cor 3:1-3	Worldly Christians are jealous and quarrel among themselves. They are not ready for solid spiritual food.
1 Cor 13:4	Love does not envy.
Gal 5:21	Envy is one of the acts of the sinful nature.
Titus 3:3	Envy is one of the characteristics of a person who is foolish, disobedient, deceived and enslaved by all kinds of passions and pleasures. It results in being hated and hating one another.
Jam 3:14-16	Envy is not from heaven. It is earthly, unspiritual, and of the devil. Where you have envy and selfish ambition, you will find disorder and every evil practice.
1 Pet 2:1-2	Envy impedes spiritual growth.

Destructive Nature of Envy

Prov 14:30	Envy rots the bones.
1 Jn 3:12	Cain was envious of his brother Abel and murdered him.
Gen 26:14	The Philistines envied Isaac and filled up the wells his father Abraham had dug.
1 Sam 18:6-12	King Saul was jealous of David and tried to kill him.
Mat 27:18	Pilate realized that envy was the reason the Jewish leaders turned Jesus over to be crucified.
Ac 5:17	The priest and Sadducees were filled with jealousy and arrested the apostles.

Counsel	
Psa 37:1	Do not be envious of those who do wrong.
Prov 3:31; 24:1-2	Do not envy a violent person. Envy is prohibited.
Prov 23:17	"Do not let your heart envy sinners."
Prov 24:1, 19	Do not envy wicked men.
1 Pet 2:1	The Christian has been purified (1:22), born again (1:23) and the word of God stands forever. Therefore, he is ordered to rid himself of envy.
Rom 15:2-3	The strong should bear with the failings of the weak. Each should please his neighbor for his good, to build him up.
Php 2:3-4	Do nothing out of selfish ambition. Consider others better than yourselves. Your attitude should be the same as that of Jesus (5-11).

The person who envies should:
1. Learn the significance of the above texts for his own experiences;
2. Recognize and confess that envy is a sin;
3. Pray for God to bless others and for good things to happen to them;
4. Seek to discover the good in other people.

FASTING

Fasting that God Honors

Jer 14:12	The fasting of the wicked is rejected by God.
Isa 58:1-5	The Israelites asked why God did not honor their fasting (1-3). God's answered that their lives were in conflict with God's plan for fasting (3-5).
Isa 58:6-13	Fasting that produces results is accompanied by practicing justice, freeing the oppressed and sharing with the needy.
Isa 58:8-14	The results of fasting God's way: you will see the light (8), you will be healed (8), your righteousness and God's glory will be visible (8), your prayers will be answered (9), the Lord will guide you and satisfy your needs (11), you will be known (11), you will experience success (12), and you will find your joy in the Lord (14).
Mat 6:16-18	Fasting is to be done in secret.

Occasions When Fasting Was Observed

Judges 20:26	In time of great sorrow
1 Sam 7:6	During a time of confessing sins
2 Sam 1:12	During a time of mourning
2 Sam 12:16	During a time of intense petitioning God in prayer
2 Chron 20:3	During a time of distress when seeking help from the Lord
Ezra 8:21-23	When seeking God's direction and protection
Ezra 10:6	When in mourning because of the sin of others, and while preparing to confront the sinners
Neh 1:4-6	In time of intense prayer and confession of sins
Neh 9:1-2	When confessing sins and dedicating oneself to the Lord
Est 4:3, 16	When facing the risk of disaster
Psa 35:13	When facing sickness
Dan 9:3	In time of prayer
Joel 1:14	In time of a sacred assembly
Joel 2:12	In time of repentance and mourning over sin

Jonah 3:5	In time of confessing and turning away from sin
Mat 4:2	Jesus fasted for 40 days when facing temptation.
Mat 6:16	Jesus spoke of "*when*" his disciples would fast, not "*if*" they would.
Mat 9:15; Lk 5:33-34	Jesus said his disciples would fast.
Ac 13:2-3	When worshiping God (2); when choosing people for a specific task (2); when commissioning and separating people for specific responsibility (3)
Ac 14:23	Prayer and fasting were part of the process of choosing and dedicating spiritual leaders.

FEAR

Gen 3:10	Fear is one of the consequences of sin. Adam and Eve were afraid after eating the forbidden fruit.
Psa 3:5-6	Loss of sleep may be the result of fear; loss of sleep may provoke fear.
Psa 27:1	"The Lord is my light and my salvation. Whom shall I fear? The Lord is the stronghold of my life. Of whom shall I be afraid?"
Psa 56:1-11	"When I am afraid, I will trust in you. In God, whose word I praise, in God I trust; I will not be afraid. What can mortal man do to me?" (3-4)
Prov 10:24	"What the wicked dreads will overtake him."
Prov 28:1	"The wicked man flees though no one pursues."
Prov 29:25	Fear of man will prove to be a snare, but whoever trusts in the Lord is kept safe.
Mat 10:26-31	Do not be afraid of those who will betray or persecute you (21-26). "Do not be afraid of those who kill the body but cannot kill the soul. Rather be afraid of the One who can destroy both soul and body in hell" (28). God cares for sparrows; people are worth more than many sparrows; so don't be afraid (31).
Rom 8:15	The Christian did not receive a spirit that makes him a slave again to fear; he received the Spirit of sonship.
2 Tim 1:7	"For God did not give us a spirit of timidity (*fear*); but a spirit of power, of love and of self-discipline."
Heb 2:14-15	Jesus, by his death, destroyed him who held the power of death (*the devil*) and freed those who were held in slavery by their fear of death.
Heb 13:5-6; Psa 118:6-7	"The Lord is my helper; I will not be afraid. What can man do to me?"
1 Pet 3:6, 12-14	Sarah is an example of a person who did what is right and did not give way to fear (6). Do not fear to suffer for doing good. Those who suffer for doing good are blessed (13-14).

| 1 Jn 4:17-18 | "There is no fear in love. But perfect love drives out fear, because fear has to do with punishment. The one who fears is not made perfect in love" (18). |

Fear is related to: Anxiety and Worry. It is the opposite of Faith.

FEAR OF GOD

Ex 20:20	The fear of God keeps one from sinning.
Deut 10:12-13	"And now, O Israel, what does the Lord your God ask of you but to fear the Lord your God, to walk in all his ways, to love him, to serve the Lord your God with all your heart and with all your soul, and to observe the Lord's commands and decrees that I am giving you today for your own good?"
Ecc 12:13	Each person should fear God and keep his commandments.
Psa 25:12	The person who fears God is instructed in the way chosen for him.
Psa 31:19	Goodness is stored up for the person who fears God.
Prov 1:7	"The fear of the Lord is the beginning of knowledge."
Prov 8:13	"To fear God is to hate evil."
Prov 9:10	"The fear of God is the beginning of wisdom."
Prov 10:27	"The fear of the Lord adds length to life."
Prov 14:26-27	"He who fears the Lord has a secure fortress, and for his children it will be a refuge. The fear of God is a fountain of life, turning a man from the snares of death."
Prov 15:16	The fear of God is worth more than wealth.
Prov 15:33	"The fear of the Lord teaches a person wisdom."
Prov 16:6	"Through the fear of the Lord a man avoids evil."
Prov 19:23	The fear of the Lord leads to life, contentment and protection.
Prov 22:4	"Humility and the fear of the Lord bring wealth, honor and life."
Prov 23:17	"Do not let your heart envy sinners, but always be zealous for the fear of the Lord."
Mat 10:28	Do not fear people who cannot kill the soul; rather fear God who can destroy both soul and body.

The Fear of God Is Illustrated in Lives	
Heb 11:7; Gen 6:13-22	Because he feared God, Noah obeyed God and built an ark to save his family.
Gen 22:12	Abraham feared God and was willing to sacrifice his son.
Gen 39:9	Joseph feared sinning against God.
1 Kg 18:12-13	When Queen Jezebel wanted to kill the Lord's prophets, Obadiah feared God and hid them.
Neh 5:14-15	Because he feared God, Nehemiah did not place a heavy burden on the people, as other governors had done.
Job 1:1, 8	Job feared God and shunned evil.
Ac 5:11	The punishment of Ananias and Sapphira produced great fear in the church.
Ac 9:31	The church grew in numbers, living in the fear of the Lord.
Ac 10:2	Cornelius was God-fearing.

FORGIVENESS OF OTHERS

Prov 17:9	Covering an offense promotes love; repeating the matter separates friends.
Prov 19:11	It is to a person's glory to overlook an offense.
Mat 6:14-15; Jam 2:13	Forgive others just like you want God to forgive you. Refuse to forgive others and God will refuse to forgive you.
Mk 11:25	When praying, forgive in order to be forgiven.
Mat 18:15-17	When a brother in Christ recognizes his sin, his sin problem is resolved. (*Recognizing sin involves: confessing sin, asking for forgiveness, and turning away from that sin*).
Mat 18:21-22; Lk 17:3-4	Each time a brother who has sinned against you repents, he should be forgiven.
Lk 17:3-10	Jesus told his disciples that if a brother sins, rebuke him; if he repents, forgive him (3-4). The disciples asked for Jesus to increase their faith (5). *(Faith is as essential to forgive as it is to receive forgiveness.)* When you forgive, you deserve no special recognition; you have only done your duty (10).
1 Cor 13:4-5	Love keeps no record of wrongs.
Eph 4:32	"Be kind and compassionate to one another, forgiving each other, just as in Christ God forgave you."
Col 3:13	"Bear with each other and forgive whatever grievances you may have against one another. Forgive as the Lord forgave you."
1 Jn 1:8-10	All people sin. Sin that is confessed is forgiven.
2 Cor 2:5-11	Forgive a repentant sinner and affirm your love for him (7-8). Where there is lack of forgiveness, Satan has the advantage (11).
Examples of Forgiveness	
Gen 33:4	Esau embraced Jacob, the brother who had stolen his blessing by lying to his father.
Gen 45:4-8; 50:19-21	Joseph forgave his brothers for selling him into slavery.

2 Sam 14:28 – 15:12	David gave Absalom partial forgiveness, allowing him to return to Jerusalem, but refusing to see him. Partial forgiveness provokes anger and rebellion. Absalom is an example.
Ac 7:60	Stephen prayed for God to forgive those who were in the act of stoning him.
2 Tim 4:16	Paul forgave those who abandoned him.
Lk 23:34	Jesus prayed for those who were in the act of crucifying him, "Father, forgive them, for they do not know what they are doing."
Eph 4:32; Col 3:13	The model for forgiveness is Christ. Forgive as the Lord forgave you.

GOD'S FORGIVENESS

Psa 32:1-5	Blessed is the person whose sin the Lord does not count against him (1-2). David was depressed when he tried to keep his sins hidden (3-4). When David confessed his sins, God forgave him and David testified, "Then I acknowledged my sin to you; and did not cover up my iniquity. I said, 'I will confess my transgressions to the Lord' – and you forgave the guilt of my sin" (5).
Psa 51:17	"A broken and contrite heart, O God, you will not despise."
Psa 86:4-7	"You are forgiving and good, O Lord, abounding in love to all who call to you" (5).
Psa 103:12	"As far as the east is from the west, so far has he removed our transgressions from us."
Prov 28:13-14	"He who conceals his sins does not prosper, but whoever confesses and renounces them finds mercy."
Isa 1:18	"'Come now, let us reason together,' says the Lord. 'Though your sins are like scarlet, they shall be as white as snow; though they are red as crimson, they shall be like wool.'"
Isa 55:6-7	"Let the wicked forsake his way and the evil man his thoughts. Let him turn to the Lord, and he will have mercy on him, and to God, for he will freely pardon."
Mat 6:12; Mk 3:28	Jesus taught us to pray for forgiveness, "Forgive us our debts, as we also have forgiven our debtors" (Mat 6:12). (*God forgives a person the same way as that person forgives others.*)
Ac 13:38-39	"Through Jesus the forgiveness of sins is proclaimed to you" (38).
Col 1:13-14	"For he (*God*) has rescued us from the dominion of darkness and brought us into the kingdom of the Son he loves, in whom we have redemption, the forgiveness of sins."
1 Jn 1:9	"If we confess our sins, he is faithful and just and will forgive us our sins and purify us from all unrighteousness."

Examples of God's Forgiveness	
Psa 32:1-5	God forgave David when he confessed his sins (2 Sam 12:13). David acknowledged his sin to God. He confessed his iniquity to the Lord and God forgave the guilt of his sin (Psa 32:5).
Psa 78:35-38	When the Israelites sinned (36-35), God was merciful; he forgave their iniquities. Time after time he restrained his anger and withheld his wrath (38).
Psa 85:2	"You forgave the iniquity of your people and covered all their sins."
Zech 3:1-5	Zechariah had a vision of the high priest in filthy clothes. They were removed and replaced with pure white garments.
Mk 2:5	Jesus forgave the paralytic man before giving him healing.
Jn 4:4-26	The Samaritan woman had been divorced five times and she was living with a man, but she was not married to him. She received "living water" from Jesus.
Lk 7:36-50	Jesus said about the penitent prostitute, "Her many sins have been forgiven – for she loved much."
Lk 15:11-31	In the parable of the Prodigal Son, the son who confessed his sins (21) was forgiven, and accepted as completely as if he had not sinned (22-24). The father represents God and reveals how God treats repentant sinners.
Lk 18:9-14	In the parable of the Pharisee and the Tax Collector, the repentant tax collector was justified.
Lk 23:43	Jesus told the murderer on the cross, "I tell you the truth, today you will be with me in paradise."
Jn 21:15-19	Peter, who denied Jesus, was forgiven and reinstated as a disciple of Jesus. Jesus then entrusted Peter with his "lambs."

1 Cor 6:9-11	"The wicked will not inherit the Kingdom of God....Neither the sexually immoral nor idolaters nor adulterers nor male prostitutes nor homosexual offenders nor thieves nor the greedy nor drunkards nor slanderers nor swindlers will inherit the Kingdom of God. And that is what some of you were. But you were washed, you were sanctified, you were justified in the name of the Lord Jesus Christ and by the Spirit of our God." *(The wicked who repent and believe in Jesus are forgiven and inherit the Kingdom of God.)*
Col 2:13	"When you were dead in your sins...God made you alive with Christ. He forgave us all our sins."

FRIENDSHIP: GOOD AND EVIL

Good Friendship

Psa 41:9; 53:12-14	Pain is felt when one is betrayed by a close friend.
Psa 119:63	The psalmist said, "I am a friend to all who fear you, to all who follow your precepts."
Prov 12:26	"A righteous man is cautious in friendship, but the way of the wicked leads them astray."
Prov 13:20	"He who walks with the wise grows wise, but a companion of fools suffers harm."
Prov 17:9	"He who covers over an offense promotes love, but whoever repeats the matter separates close friends."
Prov 17:17	"A friend loves at all times."
Prov 18:24	"There is a friend who sticks closer than a brother."
Prov 27:6	"Wounds from a friend can be trusted."
Prov 27:10	"Do not forsake your friend and the friend of your father."

Examples of Friendship

Ruth 1:16	Ruth was a friend to her mother-in-law.
1 Sam 20:17, 42	David and Jonathan are an example of friendship.
1 Kg 5:1	King Hiram of Tyre was a friend to David. After David's death, he reached out to David's son Solomon.
Rom 16:4; 2 Cor 2:13; Php 1:3; 2:25; 2 Tim 1:16	Paul was a true friend to his companions.

Friendships to Avoid

Ex 23:2	"Do not follow the crowd in doing wrong."
Psa 1:1	"Blessed is the man who does not walk in the counsel of the wicked or stand in the way of sinners or sit in the seat of mockers."

Prov 1:10-15	Do not give in to sinners (10); do not go along with them (15).
Prov 13:20	"He who walks with the wise grows wise, but a companion of fools suffers harm."
Prov 18:24	"A man of many companions may come to ruin." (*The desire for many friends brings danger.*)
Prov 22:24-25	"Do not make friends with a hot-tempered man, do not associate with one easily angered, or you may learn his ways and get yourself ensnared."
Prov 23:20	"Do not join those who drink too much wine or gorge themselves on meat."
Rom 16:17-18	Keep away from those who cause divisions and who put obstacles in the way of others that are contrary to biblical teaching.
1 Cor 5:9-13	Do not associate with anyone who calls himself a brother in Christ but is sexually immoral, or greedy, or a slanderer, or a drunkard, or a swindler (11).
1 Cor 15:33	"Bad company corrupts good character."
2 Cor 6:14-18	"Do not be yoked together with unbelievers" (14).
2 Tim 3:5	Have nothing to do with those who pretend to be Christians, but who live impure lives and deny the power of God.

GAMBLING

Casting Lots to Discover God's Will

Lev 16:8-10	Aaron was to cast lots to determine which of two goats was to be sacrificed to the Lord as a sin offering and which was to be the scapegoat.
Num 26:55-56; 33:54; 34:13; 36:2	Moses instructed that the Promise Land was to be divided among the tribes by casting lots.
Jos 14:2; 18:6-11; 19:1-51	After Joshua led the Israelites to conquer the Promise Land, the inheritances of the tribes were assigned by lot, as the Lord had commanded through Moses.
1 Sam 14:41-42	Saul asked God to reveal through the casting of lots who had disobeyed his orders.
Prov 16:33	Casting of lots was used to determine the will of God.
Ac 1:26	After Jesus' ascension, his followers cast lots to determine who would replace Judas as an apostle.

Casting Lots to Show Impartiality

1 Chr 24:5,7, 31; 25:8-9; 26:13-16	David showed impartiality in selected men for assignments by selecting them by lots.
Ne 10:34	Lots were cast to determine when each family would bring wood to the Temple to burn on the altar of the Lord.
Ne 11:1	To repopulate Jerusalem, lots were cast and one out of each ten families moved to the city.
Prov 18:18	"Casting the lot settles disputes and keeps strong opponents apart."
Lk 1:9	Priest Zechariah was chosen by lot, according to the custom of the priesthood, to go into the Temple of the Lord and burn incense.

Casting Lots by Non-Believers in God

Jon 1:7	When Jonah was on the ship during the storm, sailors cast lots to find out who was responsible for their calamity. The lot fell on Jonah.

Psa 22:18; Mat 27:35; Lk 23:34; Jn 19:24	The psalmist prophesied that the Messiah's clothes would be divided by the casting of lots. After the Roman solders had crucified Jesus, they divided his clothing by casting lots.
Eze 21:21-22	Ezekiel prophesied that the king of Babylon would arrive at the junction of two roads and he would cast lots to determine which direction to go.
Est 3:7; 9:24	When Ester was queen, Haman cast lots to select a day and month to kill the Jews, whom he considered his enemies.
Scriptural Principles Related to Gambling	
Ex 20:17	The 10th Commandment prohibits God's people from coveting another's possessions. *(Gambling derives from coveting; it is the attempt to obtain the resources of others without their receiving anything of value in return.)*
Prov 12:11; 14:23; 18:9; 21:5; Col 3:22-24; 1 Thes 4:11; 2 Thes 3:10; 1 Tim 5:8	God plans for His people to invest their time and energy into work that supplies their needs and those of their families. Scripture exhorts industriousness and admonishes against slothfulness. *(Gambling seeks to obtain one's needs without honorable work; therefore, the gambler substitutes God's plan to work, for a plan that promotes slothfulness. Gambling goes against God's work ethics.)*
Mat 6:25-34; Phil 4:19; Heb 13:5	God wants His people to look to Him as their provider. *(To engage in gambling indicates a lack of trust in God's provisions.)*
Phil 4:11-12; 1 Tim 6:6; Heb 13:5	God wants His people to be content with the material blessings they receive from His hand. *(To engage in gambling indicates a dissatisfaction with God's provision.)*
Mat 7:12	Jesus commanded, "Do to others what you would have them do to you." *(The gambler violates this command; he desires for others to suffer losses he himself does not want to suffer.)*
Mk 12:31	Jesus commanded, "Love your neighbor as yourself." *(The gambler violates this command; for one person to win at gambling, others must suffer losses.)*

1 Tim 6:9-10	Paul warns that people who want to get rich fall into temptation and into harmful desires that plunge them into ruin, and that the love of money is a root of all kinds of evil. *(Gambling is undergirded by a "get-rich-quick" appeal.)*
Rom 3:8	Paul condemns the idea that a person may do evil and good will result. *(This is an argument against religious organizations, charities or governments sponsoring gambling in order to use the profits for a good purpose.)*
1 Thes 5:22; 1 Cor 6:18; 15:33; 2 Tim 2:22	Believers in Jesus are to avoid temptation, and they are to flee from temptation. *(Gambling typically takes place in environments that are surrounded by temptations and opportunities to participate in corrupting vices.)*
2 Pet 2:19	A person is a slave to whatever mastered him. *(Gambling is addictive, and this addiction ruins families and wrecks people's financial security.)*
Rom 13:1-5	The God-ordained purpose of government is to protect the welfare of its citizens and to suppress evil. *(However, state-sanctioned gambling victimizes its citizens and promotes a vice that brings many of them to destruction.)*
Mat 25:14-30	The Parable of the Talents teaches that people are responsible before God for how they invest the resources entrusted to them. People are stewards of all the possessions with which God entrusted them. *(Money spent on gambling is almost always a certain-negative return. Money spent on gambling is poor stewardship of the resources God has given us. Such money could have been invested more securely, or it could have been spent for a positive purpose.)*

    Gambling is staking financial resources, or property, or something of value on a mere chance. The outcome depends on chance or accident. Gambling involves the desire to obtain something for nothing, without rendering service or exchange of goods.

    In the Old Testament, and in Acts 1:26, casting of lots was sometimes used to determine God's will. After the coming of the Holy Spirit in Acts 2, casting of lots was never again used to determine God's will.

In the Old Testament, impartiality was exercised in giving people responsibility or work assignments by casting lots.

The Bible does not mention casting of lots in a gambling situation; except, when solders, at the foot of the cross, cast lots to determine who would receive the clothes of Jesus.

The fact that the Bible is silent on the subject matter of gambling cannot be used as an argument that God is neutral on the subject. The Bible is also silent on the subjects of rape, suicide, sex slavery, racketeering, drug additions, and embezzlement; however, biblical principles clearly condemn these actions.

The Bible does not speak on the subject of gambling; however, biblical teachings mentioned in the above chart imply that gambling is contrary to God's plan for his people.

Gambling is related to: Addictions, Contentment, Habits that Enslave a Person, Change to Overcome Sin, Work, and Covetousness.

GIVING

Giving to God

Mal 3:7-10	Do not rob God of his tithes and offerings.
1 Cor 16:1-2	For the church collection, "On the first day of every week, each one of you should set aside a sum of money in keeping with his income."
2 Cor 9:6-7	"Whoever sows sparingly will also reap sparingly. Whoever sows generously will also reap generously. Each man should give what he has decided in his heart to give, not reluctantly or under compulsion, for God loves a cheerful giver."

Giving to Other People

Lev 25:35	One should relieve the poor needy brother, even if he is a stranger or foreigner.
Deut 15:7	Do not harden your heart nor shut your hand against a poor brother.
Prov 14:21	"He who despises his neighbor sins, but blessed is he who is kind to the needy."
Prov 19:17	"He who is kind to the poor lends to the Lord, and he will reward him for what he has done."
Prov 22:9	"A generous man will himself be blessed, for he shares his food with the poor."
Mat 5:7	"Blessed are the merciful, for they will be shown mercy."
Mat 6:1-4	Do not give in such a way as to be seen by people. If you do, you will have no reward from God. Give in secret.
Mat 19:21	Jesus told the rich young man to sell his possessions and give to the poor, and he would have treasure in heaven.
Mat 25:34-46	Whatever we do for the least of God's children is done for Jesus (35, 40).
Lk 6:27-28	"Do good to those who hate you."

Gal 6:9-10	"Let us not become weary in doing good, for at the proper time we will reap a harvest if we do not give up. Therefore, as we have opportunity, let us do good to all people, especially to those who belong to the family of believers."
1 Tim 6:17-19	The rich should be generous and willing to share.
1 Jn 3:16-18	"If anyone has material possessions and sees his brother in need but has no pity on him, how can the love of God be in him? Dear children, let us not love with words or tongue but with actions and in truth."
Examples of Giving	
Lk 21:1-4	Jesus praised the poor widow in the Temple for her sacrificial gift. Though her gift was small compared to others, Jesus said that she had given more than all the others.
2 Cor 8:1-5	The Macedonian Christians gave generosity, even though they were extremely poor. They gave as much as they were able, even beyond their ability.

GOD'S WILL

	God's Will Described
Mat 6:10	Jesus taught his followers to pray, "Your will be done on earth as it is in heaven." (*God's will is being done when he is being obeyed.*)
Rom 12:1-2	God's will is described as good, pleasing and perfect.
	Discovering God's Will
Psa 40:8	"I desire to do your will, O my God; your law is within my heart."
Psa 143:10	The psalmist prayed, "Teach me to do your will, for you are my God; may your good Spirit lead me on level ground."
Mat 6:10	Jesus taught his followers to pray, "Your kingdom come, your will be done on earth as it is in heaven."
Mat 26:42	Jesus prayed for God's will to be done in his life.
Rom 12:1-2	Present your bodies as a living sacrifice; be not conformed to this world ; but be transformed by the renewing of your mind. Then you will experience God's good, pleasing and perfect will.
Eph 6:6	Be like slaves of Christ, doing the will of God from your heart.
Jam 4:13-16	When making plans for the future (13-14), a person should say, "If it is the Lord's will, we will live and do this or that."
	Results of Doing God's Will
Mat 12:50	Whoever does the will of God the Father is a member of Jesus' family.
Heb 13:20-21	A prayer, "May the God of peace, who...brought back from the dead our Lord Jesus, that great Shepherd of the sheep, equip you with every thing good for doing his will, and may he work in us what is pleasing to him, through Jesus Christ, to whom be glory for ever and ever. Amen."
1 Jn 2:17	The person who does the will of God lives forever.

HABITS

Prov 19:19	"A hot-tempered man must pay the penalty. If you rescue him, you will have to do it again." (*A person should pay the penalty for habitual wrongdoing.*)
Jer 13:23	The person who is accustomed to doing evil, cannot do good.
Jer 22:21-22	Continually doing wrong results in punishment.
Rom 6 – 7	Do not continue sinful habits (6:1-2). Our old self was crucified with Jesus so that we should no longer be slaves to sin (6:5-7). Count yourselves dead to sin but alive to God (6:11). Choose to whom you will be a slave: to sin or to obedience (6:16). At one time you offered the parts of your body in slavery to impurity; now, offer them in slavery to righteousness (6:19). Paul knew what was right and couldn't do it; knew what was wrong and kept doing it (7:15-16). The rescue from being a slave to sin comes through Jesus Christ (7:24-25). Through Christ Jesus the law of the Spirit of life sets us free from the law of sin and death (8:1-2).
Gal 5:16-21	Live by the Spirit and you will not gratify the desires of the sinful nature (16). Acts of the sinful nature are listed (6:19-21). The fruit of the Spirit is listed (6:22-26).
2 Pet 2:14, 19	A person is a slave to whatever has mastered him (19).

Habits are related to: Addictions, and Change to Overcome Sin.

HOMOSEXUALITY

Gen 19:4-5	The men of Sodom were determined to have sex with Lot's male visitors. God punished the city with destruction.
Jude 7	"Sodom and Gomorrah and the surrounding towns gave themselves up to sexual immorality and perversion. They serve as an example of those who suffer the punishment of eternal fire."
Lev 18:22	"Do not lie with a man as one lies with a woman; that is detestable."
Lev 20:13	Homosexual acts are detestable. Those who practice them should be put to death.
Deut 23:17-18	Cultural religious prostitution is prohibited. This included homosexual prostitutes. Cultural prostitutes, including male homosexual prostitutes, were connected to corrupted religions.
Rom 1:18-32	Homosexuality is one of the results of idolatry (22-27). It is an indecent act and perversion of natural relations (27). It results in a depraved mind, is wrong (28), and will result in deserved punishment (27). Those who do such things deserve death; nevertheless, they continue to do them and approve of those who practice them (32).
2 Thes 2:10-12	People perish because they refuse to love the truth, which results in their being saved. For this reason, God sends them a delusion so that they will believe the lie and delight in wickedness.
1 Cor 6:9-11	People who are sexually immoral, adulterers, male prostitutes, and homosexual offenders will not inherit the Kingdom of God (9). It is possible for such people to be washed, sanctified and justified in the name of the Lord Jesus Christ and by the Spirit of God (11).
Gal 5:16	A person who lives by the Holy Spirit will not gratify the desires of the sinful nature.

Homosexuality is related to: Addictions, Sexual Immorality, Habits, God's Forgiveness, Lying, and Change to Overcome Sin.

Conclusions:
1. It is a sin to practice homosexual acts (Lev 18:22; Rom 1:26-32).
2. Jesus Christ is the answer for this sin (1 Cor 6:11). He offers salvation, forgiveness and cleansing from sin; an opportunity to take off sinful actions in order to put on godly actions; and the ability to restructure one's life.
3. The homosexual needs to completely reconstruct his life, because homosexuality is a sin that enslaves a person to addiction.
4. Fruits which give evidence to the fact that one has repented from the sin of homosexuality:
    4.1 Avoiding socializing with those who practice homosexuality (1 Cor 15:33).
    4.2 Reorganizing one's activities in order to avoid temptation.
    4.3 A complete reconstruction of one's life, with the power of the Holy Spirit, in order to conform to biblical principles.
    4.4 Give less emphasis to sexual experiences. For many homosexuals, the emphasis on sex becomes a form of idol worship.
    4.5 Refrain from being sexually active or learn to show love to a spouse of the opposite sex.

HONESTY

Ex 23:7	Have nothing to do with a false charge and do not punish an honest person.
Prov 3:27-28	Be prompt in making payments.
Jam 5:4	The unpaid wages of workmen cry out to God against the oppressor.
Lev 19:35-36	Use honest standards when measuring or weighing.
Deut 25:13-16	Moses told the Israelites to have accurate and honest weights and measures, so that they might live long in the land the Lord their God was giving them. The Lord detests anyone who deals dishonestly.
Psa 101:7-8	No one who practices deceit will dwell in God's house. No one who speaks falsely will stand in God's presence.
Prov 12:17	"A truthful witness gives honest testimony, but a false witness tells lies."
Prov 12:22	"The Lord detests lying lips, but he delights in people who are truthful."
Prov 16:11	"Honest scales and balances are from the Lord."
Prov 20:7	The righteous person leads a blameless life. His children are blessed.
Prov 24:26	"An honest answer is like a kiss on the lips."
Jer 5:1	The Lord God was planning on allowing the Babylonians to bring divine judgment on Jerusalem. The Lord told Jeremiah that if he could find one person who dealt honestly and sought the truth, the Lord would forgive the city. Just one honest person, and God would have saved the city of Jerusalem.
Rom 1:18	God's wrath is against the wicked who suppress the truth.
1 Cor 13:6	Love rejoices with the truth.
2 Cor 8:21	Paul and his companions took pains to do what was right; both in the eyes of the Lord and also in the eyes of men.
Eph 4:15	Speak the truth in love.
Eph 4:25	Put off falsehood and speak truthfully.

Eph 6:14	The belt of truth is part of the armor of God.
Php 4:8	Think about what is true.
2 Thes 2:10-13	Sinners perish because they refuse to love and believe the truth. Belief in the truth brings salvation.

Honesty is the opposite of Lying.

IDOLATRY

	Prohibited
Ex 20:4-5	Do not make an idol for yourself. Do not bow down to them or worship them.
Lev 19:4	"Do not turn to idols or make gods of cast metal for yourselves."
Lev 26:1	"Do not make idols or set up an image or a sacred stone for yourselves, and do not place a carved stone in your land to bow down before it."
Deut 4:16-18	"Do not become corrupt and make for yourselves an idol, an image of any shape, whether formed like a man or a woman, or like any animal on earth or any bird that flies in the air, or like any creature that moves along the ground or any fish in the waters below."
Deut 5:8-9	"You shall not make for yourself an idol in the form of anything in heaven above or on the earth beneath or in the waters below. You shall not bow down to them or worship them; for I, the Lord your God, am a jealous God."
Deut 7:25	Before entering the promised land, Moses warned the Israelites to burn the images of their gods. Do not take it for yourselves, or you will be ensnared by it. It is detestable to the Lord your God.
Deut 11:16	"Be careful, or you will be enticed to turn away and worship other gods and bow down to them. Then the Lord's anger will burn against you."
1 Sam 12:21	"Do not turn away after useless idols. They can do you no good, nor can they rescue you, because they are useless."
Isa 44:9-17	"All who make idols are nothing, and the things they treasure are worthless" (9).
Isa 45:20	People are ignorant who worship idols and who pray to gods that cannot save.
Hos 4:12	Idolatry is a form of spiritual prostitution.
Jonah 2:8	Those who worship worthless idols forfeit the grace that could be theirs.

Hab 2:18	"Of what value is an idol, since a man has carved it? Or an image that teaches lies?"
1 Cor 6:9	Idolaters will not inherit the Kingdom of Heaven.
Rev 21:8	The place for idolaters is the fiery lake of burning sulfur.
Rev 22:15	Idolaters will be outside of Heaven.
Things or Attitudes that Are Considered as Idolatry	
Ex 32:3-6 with Psa 106:19-20	Using an idol to worship the Lord God is idolatry.
1 Sam 15:23	Arrogance is like the evil of idolatry.
Psa 135:15-18	Idols are made by the hands of men. They have mouths, but cannot speak; eyes, but cannot see; ears, but cannot hear; noses, but cannot smell; hands, but cannot feel; feet, but cannot walk. Those who make them or who trust in them will be like them.
Rom 1:23-25	Fools exchange the glory of God for images made to look like people and animals (23). They exchange the truth of God for a lie and worship and serve created things rather than the Creator (25).
Gal 5:20	Idolatry is included in the list of the acts of the sinful nature.
Eph 5:5; Col 3:5	Greed is idolatry.
Ac 17:29	Idol worshipers consider that the divine being is like gold or silver or stone; images made by man's design and skill.
Our Responsibility	
Psa 24:4	The person with clean hands and a pure heart does not lift up his soul to an idol.
1 Cor 10:14-20	Flee from idolatry (14). Do not participate in activities and ceremonies that involve idolatry (19-20).
Col 3:5	Put to death whatever belongs to your earthly nature. Included in the list is greed, which is idolatry.
1 Jn 5:21	Keep yourselves from idols.

BECOMING LIKE JESUS

Christlikeness Should be the Ultimate Aim of Each Christian

Rom 8:29-30	Every Christian is predestined to be conformed to the likeness of Jesus, that he might be the firstborn among many brothers.
2 Cor 3:18	We who reflect the Lord's glory are being transformed into his likeness with ever-increasing glory. This comes from the Lord, who is the Spirit.
Eph 4:22-24	"You were taught...to put off your old self, which is being corrupted by its deceitful desires; to be made new in the attitude of your minds; and to put on the new self, created to be like God in true righteousness and holiness."
Col 3:9-10	"You have taken off your old self with its practices and have put on the new self, which is being renewed in knowledge in the image of its Creator."
2 Pet 1:3-4	"His divine power has given us everything we need for life and godliness....Through these he has given us his very great and precious promises, so that through them you may participate in the divine nature and escape the corruption in the world caused by evil desires."
1 Jn 2:6	"Whoever claims to live in him must walk as Jesus did."

Jesus Expects His Followers to Imitate Him

Mat 16:24	Jesus told his disciples, "If anyone would come after me, he must deny himself and take up his cross and follow me."
Jn 13:2-15	Jesus modeled for his disciples as he washed their feet (2-11). Then he told them to follow his example (12-15).
Jn 13:34-35	Jesus said, "Love one another. As I have loved you, so you must love one another" (34).

Jn 15:9-12	Jesus said that just as the Father loved him, so he had loved his disciples. They were to remain in his love and obey his commands, just as he had obeyed his Father's commands and remains in his love (9-11). He commanded that they love each other as he loved them (12).
Paul Instructs the Christians to Imitate Jesus	
Rom 6:10-12	"The death he (*Jesus*) died, he died to sin once for all; but the life he lives, he lives to God. In the same way, count yourselves dead to sin but alive to God in Christ Jesus."
Rom 15:1-3	"Each of us should please his neighbor for his good, to build him up. For even Christ did not please himself" (2-3).
1 Cor 11:1	Paul told his fellow Christians, "Follow my example, as I follow the example of Christ."
Eph 5:1-2	"Be imitators of God.....Live a life of love, just as Christ loved us and gave himself up for us as a fragrant offering and sacrifice to God."
Christians Are to Imitate Jesus' Self-Sacrificing Attitude	
Php 2:3-8	Do nothing out of selfish ambition or vain conceit. Consider others better than yourselves. You should not look only to your own interest, but also to the interest of others. Have the same attitude as that of Jesus Christ.
1 Pet 2:18-23	"If you suffer for doing good and you endure it, this is commendable before God. To this you were called, because Christ suffered for you, leaving you an example, that you should follow in his steps" (20-21).
1 Jn 3:16-18	"Jesus Christ laid down his life for us. We ought to lay down our lives for our brothers."
Examples of Those Who Imitated Jesus	
1 Cor 11:1	Paul said, "Follow my example, as I follow the example of Christ."
1 Thes 1:6-7	Paul told the Thessalonian Christians, "You became imitators of us and of the Lord....And so you became a model to all the believers in Macedonia and Achaia."

\	**Christians Have the Hope of One Day Being Conformed to Jesus' Image**
1 Cor 15:49	In the context of speaking about the resurrection, Paul says, "And just as we have born the likeness of the earthly man, so we shall also bear the likeness of the man from heaven."
Php 3:12, 20-21	Paul said, "I press on to take hold of that for which Christ Jesus took hold of me" (12). "We eagerly await a Savior from there (*heaven*), the Lord Jesus Christ, who, by the power that enables him to bring everything under control, will transform our lowly bodies so that they will be like his glorious body" (20-21).
1 Jn 3:2-3	"Now we are children of God, and what we will be has not yet been made known. But we know that when he appears, we shall be like him."

	LAZINESS
Prov 6:6-11	Sluggard, learn from the ant (6-9). A little sleep, a little slumber, a little folding of the hands to rest, and poverty and scarcity will come to you.
Prov 10:5	"He who sleeps during harvest is a disgraceful son."
Prov 12:11	"He who works his land will have abundant food, but he who chases fantasies lacks judgment."
Prov 13:4	"The sluggard craves and gets nothing, but the desires of the diligent are fully satisfied."
Prov 15:19	"The way of the sluggard is blocked with thorns."
Prov 19:15	"Laziness brings on deep sleep, and the shiftless man goes hungry."
Prov 20:4	"A sluggard does not plow in season, so at harvest time he finds nothing."
Prov 20:13	"Do not love sleep or you will grow poor; stay awake and you will have food to spare."
Prov 21:25-26	"The sluggard's cravings will be the death of him, because his hands refuse to work. All day long he craves for more."
Prov 24:30-34	The sluggard will come to poverty.
Prov 26:16	"The sluggard is wiser in his own eyes than seven men who answer discreetly."

LISTENING

	Listening
Ex 18:24	Moses listened when his father-in-law gave him good advice.
Deut 18:15, 19	Listen to the prophet who speaks God's Words.
Ne 8:3	The people listened when Ezra read the Book of the Law.
Prov 5:1-2	Listen well to words of insight, wisdom and prudent counsel.
Prov 12:15	A wise person listens to advice.
Prov 15:31-32	Listening to rebuke gives one understanding and makes him at home among the wise; ignoring rebuke is the same as despising oneself.
Prov 19:20	To become wise, listen to advice.
Prov 22:17	Listen to the sayings of the wise.
Jam 1:19	"Everyone should be quick to listen, slow to speak and slow to become angry."
Jam 1:22-23	Don't just listen to God's word; obey it.
	Not Listening
Lev 26:18	People who do not listen to God will be punished.
Deut 13:3	Do not listen to the prophet or dreamer who disagrees with God's Word.
1 Sam 2:25	Eli's sons refused to listen to their father's rebuke.
Prov 5:13-14	The one who does not listen to teachers is destined to ruin.
Prov 15:31-32	Ignoring rebuke is the same as despising oneself.
Prov 18:13	He who answers before listening is foolish.
Mat 10:14	God's spokes-persons should not persist with people who refuse to listen to them.
	Listening to Wrong Advice
Gen 3:17	Adam was cursed because he listened to his wife and disobeyed God.

1 Kg 12:15-16	King Jeroboam refused to listen to the people but listened to advice given by inexperienced counselors, and the nation of Israel became divided.
Prov 17:4	"A wicked man listens to evil lips; a liar pays attention to a malicious tongue."
Prov 21:28	Destruction comes to those who listen to false witnesses.
Rom 16:17-18	"Watch out for those who cause divisions and put obstacles in your way that are contrary to the teaching you have learned. Keep away from them. For such people are not serving our Lord Christ, but their own appetites. By smooth talk and flattery they deceive the minds of naive people."
2 Tim 2:14	Those who listen to quarreling about words come to ruin.

LOVE

God's Love

Jn 3:16	God loved; he gave his Son. (*Love is giving.*)
Gal 2:20	The Son of God loved and gave himself.
1 Jn 4:9-11	God loved us and sent his Son as an atoning sacrifice for our sins.

Reasons to Love

Mat 25:34-40	The person who attends to the needs of others is doing it unto Christ.
Jn 13:34-35	Jesus commanded, "Love one another. As I have loved you, so you must love one another. By this all men will know that you are my disciples, if you love one another."
1 Cor 13:1-3	Love is essential; a person is nothing without it.
Gal 5:13-15	"The entire law is summed up in a single command: Love your neighbor as yourself" (14).
1 Pet 4:8	"Above all, love each other deeply, because love covers over a multitude of sins."
1 Jn 4:19-20	"We love because he first loved us. If anyone says, 'I love God,' yet hates his brother, he is a liar. For anyone who does not love his brother, whom he has seen, cannot love God, whom he has not seen."
1 Jn 4:21	God has given us this command, "Whoever loves God must also love his brother."

Love Described

1 Cor 13:4-7	"Love is patient, love is kind. It does not envy, it does not boast, it is not proud. It is not rude, it is not self-seeking, it is not easily angered, it keeps no record of wrongs. Love does not delight in evil but rejoices with the truth. It always protects, always trusts, always hopes, always perseveres."

	Husband's Love for Wife
Eph 5:25-28	"Husbands, love your wives, just as Christ loved the church and gave himself up for her to make her holy....In this same way, husbands ought to love their wives as their own bodies. He who loves his wife loves himself."
	Inferior Kind of Love
Mat 5:43-48	"You have heard that it was said, `Love your neighbor and hate your enemy.' But I tell you: Love your enemies and pray for those who persecute you, that you may be sons of your Father in heaven" (43-45). "Be perfect, therefore, as your heavenly Father is perfect" (48).
Mat 22:39	"Love your neighbor as yourself."

For the Christian, love is a command to be obeyed, not an emotion to be acted upon.

LUST

Gen 3:6	Eve's sin began with lusting after the forbidden fruit.
Ex 20:17	"You shall not covet."
Prov 6:23-35	Warning to not lust after an immoral woman (25).
Mat 5:27-30	Looking at a woman with the intent to fantasize sex with her is adultery in the heart (28). Drastic spiritual surgery may be required (29-30).
Rom 8:5-8	"Those who live according to the sinful nature have their minds set on what that nature desires; but those who live in accordance with the Spirit have their minds set on what the Spirit desires."
Rom 13:14	"Don't think about how to gratify the desires of the sinful nature."
Gal 5:16	"Live by the Spirit and you will not gratify the desires of the sinful nature."
Eph 2:3	Those who gratify the cravings of our sinful nature and follow its desires and thoughts are objects of God's wrath.
1 Thes 4:3-6	"It is God's will that you should be sanctified: that you should avoid sexual immorality; that each of you should learn to control his own body in a way that is holy and honorable, not in passionate lust like the heathen who do not know God....The Lord will punish men for all such sins.....For God did not call us to be impure, but to live a holy life."
Tit 2:11-12	The grace of God that brings salvation teaches us to say "No" to ungodliness and worldly passions and to live self-controlled lives.
1 Pet 1:14-16	Don't conform to evil desires. Be holy in all you do.

LYING

	God Does Not Lie
Prov 6:17-19	The Lord hates a lying tongue and a lying false witness.
Tit 1:2	God does not lie.
Heb 6:18	It is impossible for God to lie.
	Lying is Prohibited
Ex 20:16	Do not give false testimony against your neighbor.
Psa 34:12-13	Whoever loves life should keep his lips from speaking lies.
Psa 120:2	The psalmist prayed for God to save him from the person with lying lips.
Prov 12:19	"Truthful lips endure forever, but a lying tongue lasts only a moment."
Prov 12:22	"The Lord detests lying lips, but he delights in men who are truthful."
Prov 19:22	"Better to be poor than to be a liar."
Prov 30:7-8	A prayer, "Keep falsehood and lies far from me."
Eph 4:25	The Christian must put off falsehood and speak truthfully.
Col 3:9	"Do not lie to each other, since you have taken off your old self with its practices and have put on the new self, which is being renewed in the image of its Creator."
	Source of Lies
Psa 10:7; 58:3	The wicked arrogant person's mouth is full of lies and threats.
Jn 8:44	When the devil lies, he speaks his native tongue. He is the father of lies.
Rom 1:25	Those who reject the truth of God exchange it for a lie.
Rom 16:17-18	Watch out for those who cause divisions and put obstacles in your way (17). "By smooth talk and flattery they deceive the minds of naive people" (18).
1 Tim 4:2	False doctrine comes from hypocritical liars.

Punishment for Lying	
Psa 5:6	God destroys those who tell lies.
Prov 12:19	"Truthful lips endure forever, but a lying tongue lasts only a moment."
Prov 19:5, 9	A false witness and one who pours out lies will be punished.
Prov 21:6	"A fortune made by a lying tongue is a fleeting vapor and a deadly snare."
Prov 29:12	"If a ruler listens to lies, all his officials become wicked."
Rev 21:8	Liars are part of the group who will burn in hell.

MARRIAGE

Gen 2:18-25	Marriage was instituted and designed by God (18-25). God said, "It is not good for man to be alone" (18). A man will leave his parents and be united to his wife and the two will become one flesh (24).
Prov 31:10-31	The description of a wife of noble character (10-31). A wife of noble character is worth far more than rubies. Her husband has full confidence in her and lacks nothing of value (10-11).
Eph 5:22-33	The relationship between husband and wife is similar to that between Christ and the church (22-32). "Wives, submit to your husbands as to the Lord" (22). "For the husband is the head of the wife as Christ is the head of the church" (23). "Now as the church submits to Christ, so also wives should submit to their husbands" (24). "Husbands, love your wives, just as Christ loved the church and gave himself up for her" (25). "Husbands ought to love their wives as their own bodies" (28). "Each one of you must love his wife as he loves himself, and the wife must respect her husband" (33).
Col 3:18-19	"Wives, submit to your husbands, as is fitting in the Lord. Husbands, love your wives and do not be harsh with them."
1 Pet 3:1-7	Wives, be submissive to you husbands (1). A wife's beauty should not come from outward adornment; it should be that of her inner self, the unfading beauty of a gentle and quiet spirit (3-4). Husbands, be considerate of your wives, and treat them with respect, so that nothing will hinder your prayers (7).
Mixed Marriages	
Gen 6:1-7	Mixed marriages (*when the sons of God went to the daughters of men and had children by them*) was one of the reasons God sent the flood.
Ex 34:16	God's people were warned not to marry spouses who worshiped other gods.

Josh 23:12-13	If God's people intermarry with those who worship other gods, they will discover that their spouses will become snares and traps for them. They will be whips on their backs and thorns in their eyes until they perish from the land which the Lord had given them.
Ezra 9:1-15	Ezra confessed the guilt of God's people who had intermarried with wives who worshiped other gods.
Neh 13:23-27	The men and women of Judah intermarried with people who worshiped other gods and were led into deep sin. God was angry with them.
2 Cor 6:14-16	Do not be yoked together with unbelievers.

Marriage is related to: Adultery, Marriage Sex, Sexual Immorality, Silent-Treatment, Reacting to Those Who Wrong You, Reconciliation, Divorce, Discipline of Parents, and Forgiveness of Others.

MARY, THE MOTHER OF JESUS

Before the Birth of Jesus

Mat 1:16	Joseph was the husband of Mary. Jesus was born to her.
Mat 1:18	Mary was pledged to be married to Joseph. She became pregnant by the Holy Spirit.
Mat 1:24-25	Joseph took Mary home as his wife, but did not have sex with her until she had given birth to Jesus.
Lk 1:26, 27, 34	Mary was a virgin pledged to be married to Joseph.
Lk 1:35	Mary became pregnant by the Holy Spirit.
Lk 1:38	Mary was the Lord's servant.
Lk 1:39, 56	Mary visited with her cousin Elizabeth for three months.
Lk 1:46-55	Mary's song.
Lk 2:5	Mary went with Joseph to be registered in the town of Bethlehem.

When Jesus Was a Baby/Child

Lk 2:6-7, 16	Mary gave birth to her baby boy and placed him in a feeding trough.
Lk 2:19	Mary meditated on the events surrounding Jesus' birth.
Lk 2:34-35	Mary heard Simeon's prophesy that she would suffer.
Mat 2:11	Mary and the child Jesus were in a home when they were visited by scholars from the east.
Mat 2:14	Joseph, Mary and the child Jesus escaped to Egypt.
Mat 2:19-23	Joseph, Mary and the child Jesus returned from Egypt and went to live in a town called Nazareth.
Lk 2:41-51	Mary was troubled in Jerusalem when 12 year old Jesus was separated from her and Joseph (44-45). She did not understand Jesus' explanation of his action (50). She meditated on what happened (51).

	When Jesus Was a Man
Jn 2:1-5	Mary was present at a wedding with Jesus and his disciples. When she tried to command Jesus, he questioned her and did not resolve the problem (3-4). Then Mary ordered the servants to obey Jesus (5). At that point, Jesus changed water to wine (9).
Jn 2:12	Mary and her other sons went, for a few days, with Jesus and his disciples to Capernaum.
Mk 3:21, 31	Mary and Jesus' brothers thought he was out of his mind and went to take him home by force.
Mk 3:34-35	Jesus gave more value to his relationship with his disciples than with his family.
Mat 13:55-56	Mary, the mother of Jesus, had other sons and daughters.
Jn 19:25-27	Mary stood near the cross when Jesus was crucified. Jesus told his disciple John to take her as his mother.
Ac 1:14	After Jesus was taken up into Heaven, Mary and her sons were in the upstairs room with other followers of Jesus.

	MASTURBATION
Mat 5:27-28	Fantasizing having forbidden sex is adultery in the heart.
Rom 13:14	Do not fantasize about how to satisfy the desires of the sinful nature.
1 Cor 6:12	Masturbation is not mentioned in the text. It is probably one of the actions that is permitted, but not beneficial. One should not be mastered by anything. *(Masturbation can become a habit that masters a person.)*
1 Cor 7:9	The choices for dealing with sexual passion are self-control or marriage. *(Masturbation is not mentioned as an alternative.)*
1 Cor 7:3-4	The husband has the duty toward his wife. The wife has the duty toward her husband. The marriage partner has the rights over a spouse's body. *(The individual does not have the rights over his own body, neither does one have the duty to self-satisfy.)*
1 Thes 4:3-6	"It is God's will that you should be sanctified: that you should avoid sexual immorality; that each of you should learn to control his own body in a way that is holy and honorable, not in passionate lust like the heathen, who do not know God."

The Bible does not speak on the subject of masturbation. However, principles found in the above texts lead me to conclude that masturbation is not part of God's plan for a person. It may be permitted, but it is not beneficial.

OBEDIENCE TO GOD'S COMMANDMENTS

1 Sam 15:22-23	Prophet Samuel told King Saul, "To obey (*God*) is better than sacrifice....For rebellion is like the sin of divination, and arrogance like the evil of idolatry. Because you have rejected the word of the Lord, he has rejected you as king."
Psa 19:7-14	The law of the Lord is perfect, trustworthy, right, radiant (7-10). In keeping it, there is great reward (11).
Psa 119:1-8	"Blessed are they...who walk according to the law of the Lord. Blessed are they who keep his statutes and seek him with all their heart" (1-2). "You have laid down precepts that are to be fully obeyed" (4).
Prov 13:13	"He who scorns instruction will pay for it, but he who respects a command is rewarded."
Mat 7:21	The only people who will enter the kingdom of heaven are those who do the will of God the Father who is in heaven.
Mat 7:24-27	Every person who hears Jesus' words and puts them into practice is like the wise man who built his house upon the rock. Everyone who does not put Jesus' words into practice is like the foolish man who built his house upon the sand.
Lk 11:28	Blessed are those who hear the word of God and obey it.
Jn 14:15	Jesus said, "If you love me, you will obey what I command."
Jn 15:10-17	Jesus said, "If you obey my commands, you will remain in my love" (10). "You are my friends if you do what I command" (14).
Jam 1:22-25	Do not merely listen to the word of God; do what it says.
1 Jn 5:2-3	To love God is to obey his commands. His commands are not burdensome.

DISCIPLINE BY PARENTS

Proper Discipline

Deut 6:4-7	Parents should talk about God's commandments to their children.
Prov 13:24	"He who spares the rod hates his son, but he who loves him is careful to discipline him."
Prov 22:6	"Train a child in the way he should go, and when he is old he will not turn from it."
Prov 22:15	The rod of discipline will drive folly far from a child.
Prov 23:13-14	"Do not withhold discipline from a child; if you punish him with the rod, he will not die. Punish him with the rod and save his soul from death."
Prov 29:15	"The rod of correction imparts wisdom, but a child left to himself disgraces his mother."
Prov 29:17	"Discipline your son, and he will give you peace; he will bring delight to your soul."
Eph 6:4	Fathers should bring up their children in the training and instruction of the Lord.
1 Tim 3:4	"He (*a pastor*) must manage his own family well and see that his children obey him with proper respect."
Heb 12:5-11	"The Lord disciplines those he loves" (6). "We have all had human fathers who disciplined us and we respected them for it" (9). Our fathers disciplined us for a little while as they thought best; but God disciplines us for our good, that we may share in his holiness" (10). "No discipline seems pleasant at the time, but painful. Later on, however, it produces a harvest of righteousness and peace for those who have been trained by it" (11).

Improper Discipline

1 Sam 3:13	Eli sinned in failing to restrain his sons. (*Eli failed to discipline his sons.*)
1 Sam 20:30-33	Saul disciplined his son Jonathan with cruel words (3). When son Jonathan questioned his father, Saul tried to kill him by hurling a spear at Jonathan (32). (*Saul gave cruel discipline.*)

Eph 6:4	"Fathers, do not exasperate your children; instead, bring them up in the training and instruction of the Lord."
Col 3:21	"Fathers, do not embitter your children, or they will become discouraged."

PEACE

	God and Peace
Isa 9:6-7	One of the prophetic names given to the coming Messiah was "Prince of Peace."
Isa 53:5	A prophetic promise: The suffering of the promised Messiah brought peace.
Rom 15:33; 16:20; 1 Cor 14:33; Php 4:9; Heb 13:20	God is a God of peace.
Gal 5:22	Peace is a fruit of the Spirit.
Mat 10:34; Lk 12:51	Jesus did not come to bring peace but division.
Eph 2:14-17	Jesus is our peace.
Jn 14:27	Jesus promised to give his peace to his disciples.
Jam 3:17	Wisdom that comes from Heaven is peace-loving.
	Responsibility to Seek Peace
Psa 34:14	Turn from evil, do good and seek peace.
Jer 29:7	The captive Jews who were transported to Babylon were told to seek the peace and prosperity of the city.
Mk 9:50	Have salt in yourselves and be at peace with each other.
Rom 12:18-19	"As far as it depends on you, live at peace with everyone. Do not take revenge."
Rom 14:19	"Make every effort to do what leads to peace and to mutual edification."
Eph 4:3	"Make every effort to keep the unity of the Spirit through the bond of peace."
Php 4:6-9	Instead of being anxious, make petitions with thanksgiving, and the peace of God which transcends human understanding will guard your hearts and minds in Christ Jesus.

Col 3:12-15	Characteristics are listed that the Christian is to achieve (12-14). "Let the peace of Christ rule in your hearts, since as members of one body you were called to peace" (15).
1 Thes 5:13	"Live in peace with each other."
Heb 12:14	Make every effort to live in peace with everyone.
1 Pet 3:10-11	Whoever loves life must seek peace and pursue it.
The Benefits of Peace	
Psa 37:37	"There is a future for the man of peace."
Prov 12:20	"There is...joy for those who promote peace."
Prov 14:30	"A heart at peace gives life to the body."
Mat 5:9	"Blessed are the peacemakers, for they will be called sons of God."
Jam 3:18	"Peacemakers who sow in peace raise a harvest of righteousness."
Those Who Experience Peace	
Lev 26:6	God promised the Israelites that if they obey his commands, he would grant peace in the land.
Psa 4:8	The psalmist could lie down and sleep in peace, because God made him dwell in peace.
Psa 37:11	"But the meek will inherit the land and enjoy great peace."
Psa 58:8	The Lord God promises peace to his people, his saints.
Psa 119:165	Those who love God's Law have great peace.
Prov 3:17	The paths of wisdom are peace.
Prov 16:7	"When a person's ways are pleasing to the Lord, he makes even his enemies live at peace with him."
Isa 26:3-4	God will keep in perfect peace the person whose mind is steadfast because he trusts in him.
Isa 32:17-18	"The fruit of righteousness will be peace; the effect of righteousness will be quietness and confidence forever" (17).
Isa 57:2	"Those who walk uprightly enter into peace; they find rest as they lie in death."

Lk 7:36-50	Jesus gave the sinful woman who anointed him with perfume forgiveness of her sins (48) and peace (50).
Rom 5:1	"Since we have been justified through faith, we have peace with God through our Lord Jesus Christ."
Rom 8:6	"The mind of sinful man is death, but the mind controlled by the Spirit is life and peace."
Lack of Peace	
Ecc 3:8	There is a time for war and a time for peace.
Isa 48:22; 57:21	There is no peace for the wicked.
Jer 6:13-14; 8:11; Eze 13:10,16	False prophets and priests promise peace when there is no peace.
Mat 10:34; Lk 12:51	Jesus did not come to bring peace but division.

	PEDOPHILIA
Lev 18:6	Sexual relations with family members are prohibited. (*Many children suffer sexual abuse from family members. Incest is prohibited.*)
Mat 18:1-14	Jesus used a child to teach that child-like-faith is necessary for entrance into the Kingdom of Heaven, and that the Father is concerned for all his little ones. Jesus declared that it would be better for a person to drown in the sea than to cause a little one to sin. (*God sees an offense against a child as a very serious offense.*)
Mk 7:21-23 Gal 5:16, 19	Live by the Spirit and you will not gratify the desires of the sinful nature. The desires of the sinful nature include: illicit sex, perversion and promiscuity. (The English word "Porno" comes from the Greek word "Porneia." Some translations use the word, "Fornication." NIV translates it as "Sexual immorality." The word refers to any illicit sexual activity. The word is present on the list of the "Acts of the Sinful Nature" (Gal 5:16-21 and on the list of evil things that come out of people's hearts (Mk 7:21-23).

There is no direct mention in the Bible about pedophilia, but the issue can be addressed with timeless principles that come from the Scripture teaching about sexual immorality and God's concern for the children.

PERSECUTION

Source of Persecution

Jn 16:3	Persecutors do such things because they have not known God the Father nor Jesus.
Jn 15:18-20, 24	Those who hate God, hate the followers of Jesus (18-19). Those who would persecute Jesus will persecute his followers (20).
Ac 13:50	Those whose zeal for God is wrongly directed will persecute those who are faithfully following Jesus.
Ac 26:9-11	Before Paul became a follower of Jesus, his zeal for God was wrongly directed toward eliminating Christians.
Gal 5:11	Preachers of the Gospel will be persecuted by those who disagree with them.

The Persecuted Can Know

Mat 5:11-12	Great is the reward in heaven for the persecuted.
Mat 13:21	The person who is similar to the rocky soil in the parable of the Sower will receive the Gospel gladly but when persecution comes, he quickly falls away.
2 Cor 4:7-9	God does not abandon the person who is being persecuted.

Desired Reactions of the Persecuted

Mat 5:11-12	Jesus said, "Blessed are you when people insult you, persecute you and falsely say all kinds of evil against you because of me. Rejoice and be glad, because great is your reward in heaven, for in the same way they persecuted the prophets who were before you."
Mat 5:44	Jesus taught, "Love your enemies and pray for those who persecute you."
Rom 12:14	"Bless those who persecute you; bless and do not curse."

1 Pet 4:13-16	"But rejoice that you participate in the sufferings of Christ, so that you may be overjoyed when his glory is revealed. If you are insulted because of the name of Christ, you are blessed, for the Spirit of glory and of God rests on you....If you suffer as a Christian, do not be ashamed, but praise God that you bear that name."
1 Pet 4:19	"So then, those who suffer according to God's will should commit themselves to their faithful Creator and continue to do good."

Persecution is related to: Afflictions and Trails.

PORNOGRAPHY

Ex 20:17	You shall not covet.
Psa 101:3	The Psalmist David would not put anything wicked before his eyes.
Prov 6:23-35	Warning to not lust after an immoral woman (25).
Isa 5:20	It will be horrible for those who call evil good and good evil.
Mat 5:27-30	Looking at a woman with the intent to fantasize having sex with her is adultery in the heart (28). Drastic spiritual surgery may be required (29-30).
Rom 8:5-8	Those who live according to the sinful nature have their minds set on what that nature desires; those who live in accordance with the Spirit have their minds set on what the Spirit desires.
Rom 12:1-2	Offer you bodies as a living sacrifice to God. Don't conform to the pattern of this world but be transformed by changing the way you think.
Rom 13:14	Don't think about how to gratify the desires of the sinful nature.
Eph 2:3	Those who gratify the cravings of our sinful nature and follow its desires and thoughts are objects of God's wrath.
Gal 5:16, 19	Live by the Spirit and you will not gratify the desires of the sinful nature. The desires of the sinful nature include: illicit sex, perversion and promiscuity.
Phil 4:8	Think about things that are pure, lovely, admirable, excellent or praiseworthy.
Col 2:8	Make sure no one takes you captive through misleading philosophy.
Col 3:2	Set you minds on things above, not on earthly things.

1 Thes 4:3-6	It is God's will that you should be sanctified: that you should avoid sexual immorality; that each of you should learn to control his own body in a way that is holy and honorable, not in passionate lust like those who do not know God. The Lord will punish men for all such sins. God did not call us to be impure, but to live a holy life.
Tit 2:11-12	The grace of God that brings salvation teaches us to say "No" to ungodliness and worldly passions and to live self-controlled lives.
1 Pet 1:14-16	Don't conform to evil desires; be holy in all you do.
1 Pet 2:12	Keep away from sinful desires.

PRIDE

Pride is Evil

1 Sam 2:3	Do not speak proudly or arrogantly; God knows and rewards deeds.
Prov 8:13	The fear of the Lord results in hating pride and arrogance.
Prov 16:5	The Lord detests the proud of heart; they will not go unpunished.
Prov 16:18-19	"Pride goes before destruction; a haughty spirit brings a fall" (18).
Prov 21:4	"Haughty eyes and a proud heart, the lamp of the wicked, are sin!"
Prov 21:24	Pride is related to arrogance and mockery.
Mk 7:21-23	Arrogance is a problem of the heart. It makes a person unclean.
Jam 4:10	"Humble yourself before the Lord, and he will lift you up."
1 Pet 5:6	"Humble yourselves, therefore, under God's mighty hand, that he may lift you up in due time."

Characteristics of Pride

1 Tim 3:6	Being conceited is a characteristic of the devil.
1 John 2:16	Boasting comes from the world.
1 Tim 6:3-4	Conceit is a characteristic of false teachers who have unhealthy interests in controversies and quarrels, and who think that godliness is a means to financial gain.
Rom 1:30	The wicked (1:18) are insolent, arrogant and boastful (1:30).

Results of Pride

Prov 11:2	"When pride comes, then comes disgrace, but with humility comes wisdom."
Prov 13:10	Pride breeds quarrels.
Prov 16:18-19	Pride brings destruction. A haughty spirit brings a fall. *(Illustrated in 2 Chro 25:18-19, the thistle considered itself equal to a cedar.)*
Prov 21:24	Pride produces arrogance and mockery.

Prov 29:23	Pride brings a person down.
Jer 43:1-2	The text gives an example of arrogant men rejecting God's Word and his messenger.
Jer 49:16	Pride in the heart results in becoming deceived.
Obadiah 3	Pride in the heart deceives people and gives them false security.
Mk 7:21-23	Arrogance makes a person unclean.
1 Tim 6:3-4	Conceit results in an unhealthy interest in controversies and quarrels.

DIVINE PROTECTION FROM ENEMIES

Deut 20:1-4	God promised the Israelites that he would go into battle with them to give them victory.
Isa 8:10	When God is with a people, an enemy's strategies and plans will fail.
Isa 8:12-13	A person should fear the Lord and not people.
Psa 3:5; 4:8	God protected the psalmist while he slept.
Psa 17:6-9	Pray for divine protection from the wicked and from one's enemies.
Psa 91:3-7, 11	The Lord protects from different kinds of danger (3-7). His angels protect us (11).
Prov 3:25-26	Do not fear, the Lord is our confidence and will protect us from traps.

QUARRELS

The Cause of Quarrels

Prov 10:12	"Hatred stirs up dissension, but love covers over all wrongs."
Prov 13:10	"Pride only breeds quarrels."
Prov 15:18	"A hot-tempered man stirs up dissension, but a patient man calms a quarrel."
Prov 16:28	"A perverse man stirs up dissension, and a gossip separates close friends."
Prov 22:10	"Drive out the mocker, and out goes strife; quarrels and insults are ended."
Prov 23:29-30	Alcohol stirs up strife.
Prov 26:21	"As charcoal to embers and as wood to fire, so is a quarrelsome man for kindling strife."
Prov 28:25	"A greedy man stirs up dissensions."
Prov 30:33	"For as churning the milk produces butter, and as twisting the nose produces blood, so stirring up anger produces strife."
1 Tim 6:4	False doctrines produce an unhealthy interest in controversies and quarrels about words that result in envy, strife, malicious talk, evil suspicions and constant friction.
Jam 3:16	Envy and selfish ambition result in disorder and evil practice.
Jam 4:1	Evil desires within a person cause fights and quarrels.

Responsibility to Avoid Quarrels

Prov 17:14	The difficulty of ending a quarrel is a reason for avoiding one.
Prov 20:3	"It is to a man's honor to avoid strife, but every fool is quick to quarrel."
Mat 5:23-24	Seek reconciliation with the person who has something against you.
Mat 5:39-40	Allow others to do you wrong.

Rom 12:18	"If it is possible, as far as it depends on you, live at peace with everyone."
2 Tim 2:14	Avoid quarreling about words.
2 Tim 2:23-25	The Lord's servant must not have anything to do with foolish and stupid arguments that produce quarrels. He must not quarrel; he must be gentle to those who oppose him.
Results of Quarrels	
Gal 5:15	"If you keep on biting and devouring each other, watch out or you will be destroyed by each other."
Jam 3:16-17	Envy and selfish ambition results in disorder and every evil practice.

REACTING TO THOSE WHO WRONG YOU

When the Wrongdoer Is a Christian Brother

Mat 18:15-17	1st Go to the one who wronged you. If he listens, the problem is resolved. 2nd If he will not listen, take one or two others along. 3rd If he refuses to listen to them, tell it to the church. 4th If he refuses to listen to the church, treat him as you would a pagan.

Forgive the Wrongdoer Who Repents

Mat 6:14-15; Jam 2:13	Forgive others just like you want God to forgive you. Refuse to forgive others and God will refuse to forgive you.
Mat 18:21-22; Lk 17:3-4	Each time a brother who has sinned against you repents, he should be forgiven.
Lk 17:3-10	Jesus told his disciples: If a brother sins, rebuke him; if he repents, forgive him (3-4). The disciples asked for Jesus to increase their faith (5). (*Faith is required, both to forgive and to receive forgiveness*).

Revenge Is Prohibited

Prov 20:22	"Do not say: 'I'll pay you back for this wrong!' Wait for the Lord."
Prov 24:29	When you are wronged by a neighbor, do not say, "I'll do to him as he has done to me; I'll pay that man back for what he did."
Rom 12:17-21	"Do not repay anyone evil for evil" (17). "Do not take revenge, my friends, but leave room for God's wrath" (19).
1 Thes 5:15	"Make sure that nobody pays back wrong for wrong. But always try to be kind to each other and to everyone else."

Protecting Life and Property Is Permitted

Ex 22:2	"If a thief is caught breaking in and is struck so that he dies, the defender is not guilty of bloodshed."

	Overcome Evil With Good
Ex 23:4-5	"If you come across your enemy's donkey wandering off, be sure to take it back to him. If you see the donkey of someone who hates you fallen down under its load, do not leave it there; be sure you help him with it."
Prov 25:21	"If your enemy is hungry, give him food to eat; if he is thirsty, give him water to drink. In doing this, you will heap burning coals on his head, and the Lord will reward you."
Mat 5:38-47	"Do not resist an evil person. If someone strikes you on the right cheek, turn to him the other also" (39). "And if someone wants to sue you and take your tunic, let him have your cloak as well" (40). "If someone forces you to go one mile, go with him two miles" (41). "Love your enemies and pray for those who persecute you" (44). "Be sons of your Father in heaven. He causes his sun to rise on the evil and the good, and sends rain on the righteous and the unrighteous" (46).
Rom 12:14	"Bless those who persecute you; bless and do not curse."
Rom 12:17-21	Do not repay anyone evil for evil" (17). "Do not be overcome by evil, but overcome evil with good" (21).
	Pursue Peace With All
Rom 12:18-21	If it is possible, as far as it depends on you, live at peace with everyone (18).

Reacting to Those Who Wrong You is related to: Anger, Bitterness, Giving Correction, Forgiveness of Others, Becoming like Jesus, Peace, Quarrels, and Reconciliation.

RECONCILIATION

Mat 5:23-24	Seek reconciliation with the brother whom you have offended.
Mat 18:15-19	Seek reconciliation with the brother who has sinned against you (15-17). Jesus is present where two or three come together in his name seeking reconciliation (19).
Lk 17:3-10	Jesus told his disciples that if a brother sins, rebuke him; if he repents, forgive him (3-4). The disciples asked for Jesus to increase their faith (5). (*Faith is essential, both to forgive and to receive forgiveness.*) When you forgive, you deserve no special recognition, you have only done your duty (10).
Mat 18:21-35; 6:14-15	It is our obligation to forgive the person who repents, just as God forgives us.

REVENGE IS PROHIBITED

	Revenge is Prohibited
Lev 19:18	"Do not seek revenge or bear a grudge against one of your people, but love your neighbor as yourself. I am the Lord."
Prov 20:22	"Do not say: 'I'll pay you back for this wrong!' Wait for the Lord, and he will deliver you."
Prov 24:28-29	When you were wronged by a neighbor, do not say, "I'll do to him as he has done to me; I'll pay that man back for what he did."
Rom 12:17-21	"Do not repay anyone evil for evil" (17). "Do not take revenge, my friends, but leave room for God's wrath" (19).
1 Thes 5:15	"Make sure that nobody pays back wrong for wrong, but always try to be kind to each other and to everyone else."
1 Pet 3:9-12	"Do not repay evil with evil or insult with insult, but with blessings, because to this you were called so that you may inherit a blessing" (9).
	Examples of Revenge
Gen 39:7-16	Potiphar's wife sought revenge against Joseph, because he refused to go to bed with her.
1 Ki 19:2	Jezebel sought revenge against the prophet Elijah.
1 Ki 22:27	Ahab sought revenge against the prophet Micaiah who prophesied against him.
Est 3:6	Haman sought revenge against Mordecia who refused to bow down before him. He also sought to destroy all the Jews, the people of Mordecai.
Eze 25:15	The Philistines dealt by revenge and took vengeance with a despiteful heart.
Mat 14:8	Herodias sought revenge against John the Baptist, who had condemned her for her sin of adultery.
Lk 4:29	The Nazarenes did not like Jesus' message and sought to kill him.
Ac 5:33	The Sanhedrin sought to kill the apostles, who had disobeyed them by continuing to speak about Jesus.

Ac 23:12	Certain Jews banded together and bound themselves under a curse to neither eat nor drink until they had killed Paul.

Revenge is related to Anger, Persecution, Forgiveness of Others, and Reaction to those Who Wrong You.

SELF-OPINION

Gen 1:31	Everything God made was very good. (*God does not make trash.*)
Mat 22:34-40	Love the Lord and love your neighbor as yourself. (*A person needs to love himself in order to love another.*)
Mk 8:36	One individual is worth more than the entire wealth of the world.
Jn 3:16	God loves each person in the world.
Rom 12:3	"Do not think of yourself more highly than you ought, but rather think of yourself with sober judgment, in accordance with the measure of faith God has given you."
2 Cor 4:7	We have treasure in jars of clay to show that power is from God and not from us. (*We have value because of the treasure God puts in us.*)
Php 2:3-4	"Do nothing out of selfish ambition or vain conceit, but in humility consider others better than yourselves. Each of you should look not only to your own interests, but also to the interests of others."
1 Pet 5:5	"Clothe yourselves with humility toward one another, because God opposes the proud but gives grace to the humble."

There are two dangers related to self-opinion: high self esteem or low self esteem.

SELF-CENTEREDNESS

Mat 20:26-28	"Whoever wants to become great among you must be your servant, and whoever wants to be first must be your slave."
Lk 9:23-25	"If anyone would come after me, he must deny himself and take up his cross daily and follow me. For whoever wants to save his life will lose it, but whoever loses his life for me will save it. What good is it for a man to gain the whole world, and yet lose or forfeit his very self?"
Rom 15:2-3	"Each of us should please his neighbor for his good, to build him up. Even Christ did not please himself."
1 Cor 10:24	"Nobody should seek his own good, but the good of others."
1 Cor 13:5	Love is not self-seeking.
Jam 3:14-16	Envy and selfish ambition does not come down from heaven but is earthly, unspiritual, of the devil. Where there is envy and selfish ambition, there is disorder and every evil practice.

SELF-CONTROL

The Ability for Self-Control Is a Gift from God

Gal 5:22-23	"But the fruit of the Spirit is...self-control."
2 Tim 1:7	God gave us a spirit of power, of love and of self-discipline.
Tit 2:11-12	The grace of God that brings salvation teaches us to live self-controlled.

Each Person Has the Responsibility to Obtain Self-Control

Prov 16:32	"Better a patient man than a warrior, a man who controls his temper than one who takes a city."
Prov 25:28	"Like a city whose walls are broken down is a man who lacks self-control."
Prov 29:11	"A fool gives full vent to his anger, but a wise man keeps himself under control."
Rom 6:12	"Therefore, do not let sin reign in your mortal body so that you obey its evil desires."
2 Cor 10:4-5	"...We take captive every thought to make it obedient to Christ."
1 Thes 4:3-6	"It is God's will that you should be sanctified: that you should avoid sexual immorality; that each of you should learn to control his own body in a way that is holy and honorable, not in passionate lust like the heathen, who do not know God."
1 Thes 5:4-8	You are not in darkness; you are sons of the light. So let us not be like others; let us be alert and self-controlled. Since we belong to the day, let us be self-controlled.
Tit 1:8	An elder (*pastor*) must be self-controlled.
Tit 2:2-6	Teach the older men to be self-controlled (2). The older women should teach what is good. They can train the younger women to be self-controlled (3-5). Encourage the young men to be self-controlled (6).
Jam 3:2	"We all stumble in many ways. If anyone is never at fault in what he says, he is a perfect man, able to keep his whole body in check."
1 Pet 1:13	"Prepare your minds for action; be self-controlled."

1 Pet 4:7	The end of all things is near. Therefore, be clear minded and self-controlled so that you can pray.
2 Pet 1:5-6	"Make every effort to add to your faith...self-control."
Examples of Self-Control	
Jer 35:1-14	The descendants of Jonadab followed their ancestor's instructions and refused to drink wine.
Dan 1:8	"But Daniel resolved not to defile himself with the royal food and wine."
1 Cor 9:27	Paul said, "No, I beat my body and make it my slave so that after I have preached to others, I myself will not be disqualified for the prize." (*In the context of 1 Cor 9:24-27, Paul is comparing himself to the athlete who competes as a runner (24, 26) and a boxer (26). Paul, just like the athlete, exercises strict control because he is in training and does not want to be disqualified.*)

SELF-PITY

	Self-Pity Is Counter-Productive
Psa 73: 2-3, 21-22	The psalmist almost slipped when he experienced self-pity (2-3). He became embittered, senseless, ignorant and beast-like (21-22).
Psa 37:1, 8	Self-pity results in fretting and becoming envious (1), becoming angry, feeling wrath and doing evil (8).
Prov 15:13	A happy heart makes the face cheerful; heartache crushes the spirit.
	Examples of the Counter-Productivity of Self-Pity
2 Sam 13:1-15	Amnon's self-pity resulted in frustration to the point of sickness (1-2), planning actions that harmed his step-sister (3-6), and wrongfully mistreating his step-sister (7-15).
1 Kg 19:4, 10-19	Elijah's self-pity resulted in fear (4), depression (4-5), despair and exaggerating the problem while refusing to see positive evidence which contradicted his negative viewpoint (10). God's solution: Elijah received a word from God and got busy fulfilling his obligations (15-19).
	Solution to Self-Pity
Psa 37:1-8	Trust in God, do good, delight in the Lord, commit your way to the Lord (3-5), wait patiently for God to act (7), and refrain from anger and turn from wrath (8).
Psa 73:17-20	Repent of self-pity and focus attention on worshiping God.
Prov 10:19; 13:3	When words are many, sin is present (10:19). Speaking rashly results in ruin (13:3). (*Be careful with what is said.*)

Self-pity provokes anger, then bitterness, then depression. Self-pity is counter-productive; it leads to self-destruction. Problems of the past become a present day disaster. Complaining only increases the misery. People experiencing self-pity spend hours talking to anyone who will listen about their complaints.

Counsel to the person who is experiencing self-pity:
- Change your habits.
- Read Psalms 73 and 37 daily until self-pity is conquered.
- Pray. Make a prayer list and spend a short time with each request. Remember 1 Peter 5:7. Some people experiencing self-pity will spend hours meditating on the problems with the assumption that they are praying. Suggestions for praying:
    - Set a timer and give two minutes to think about the problem. This prevents one from increasing bitterness and becoming incapacitated.
    - Set the timer again. Read 1 Peter 5:7 and pray about the problem for two minutes.
    - Get up from praying and get active.
- Get busy with activity which will result in fulfilling one's obligations.

MARRIAGE SEX

Gen 1:28-31	Everything God made was very good. This includes sex (31). Before Adam and Eve sinned, God had commanded the couple to be fruitful and increase in number (28).
Prov 5:18-20	May you rejoice in the wife of your youth; may her breast satisfy you always; may you ever be captivated by her love.
1 Cor 7:3-5	Both husband and wife should fulfill their marital duty to their spouse (3). A person's body belongs to his/her spouse (4). Refrain from sex only with mutual consent; refraining can lead to temptation (5).
Heb 13:4	Marriage should be honored by all and the marriage bed kept pure. God will judge the adulterer and all the sexually immoral.

SEXUAL IMMORALITY

Sexual Immorality is Prohibited

Ex 20:14	"You shall not commit adultery."
Lev 20:10-12, 17-21	Specifically mentioned as prohibited: sex with another man's wife, with father's wife, with daughter-in-law, with the same sex, with a woman and her mother, with an animal; and incest with sister, aunt or brother's wife.
Mal 2:13-16	The Lord is a witness to marriage alliances. Do not be unfaithful to the marriage covenant. God hates divorce.
Mat 5:31-32	A person is guilty of adultery if he marries someone who is divorced without scriptural reasons.
Mat 19:9; Rom 7:2-3	The person who divorces a faithful spouse in order to marry another is guilty of adultery.
Heb 13:4	God will judge the adulterer and all the sexually immoral.
Jude 6-7	Sodom and Gomorrah gave themselves up to sexual immorality and perversion. They serve as examples of those who suffer the punishment of eternal fire.

Warnings

Prov 5:1-23	Warning against adultery. Counsel to rejoice in the wife of your youth.
Prov 6:23-35	Warning to not lust after an immoral woman (25). Adultery brings certain punishment (29). A person who commits adultery lacks judgment and the result is self-destruction (32).
Prov 7:5-27	Warning against the adulteress. The adulteress' snare leads to disaster. She is a pathway to the grave (27).
Mat 5:27-30	Looking at a woman with the intent to fantasize having sex with her is adultery in the heart (28). Drastic spiritual surgery may be required (29-30).

Avoid Sexual Immorality

Gen 39:12	Joseph fled from Potiphar's wife when she tempted him to go to bed with her.
Prov 2:16-18	Wisdom will protect a man from an adulterous woman.

Prov 4:27	"Keep your foot from evil."
Prov 5:1-12	Keep to a path far from an adulteress; do not go near her door (8).
Mat 15:19	"For out of the heart come evil thoughts, murder, adultery, sexual immorality....These are what make a man `unclean.'"
1 Cor 3:16-17	"You yourselves are God's temple; God's Spirit lives in you. If anyone destroys God's temple, God will destroy him."
1 Cor 6:12-20	The body is not meant for sexual immorality, but for the Lord (13). Flee from sexual immorality (18). Honor God with your body (20).
Gal 5:16-18	Live by the Spirit, and you will not gratify the desires of the sinful nature.
Eph 5:3-17	"Among you there must not be even a hint of sexual immorality, or of any kind of impurity" (3). "Live as children of light" (8). "Have nothing to do with the fruitless deeds of darkness, but rather expose them" (11). "Be careful, then, how you live" (15).
Col 3:5-6	"Put to death, therefore, whatever belongs to your earthly nature: sexual immorality, impurity, lust, evil desires."
1 Thes 4:3-7	"It is God's will that you should be sanctified: that you should avoid sexual immorality; that each of you should learn to control his own body in a way that is holy and honorable, not in passionate lust like the heathen, who do not know God; and that in this matter no one should wrong his brother or take advantage of him. The Lord will punish men for all such sins....God did not call us to be impure, but to live a holy life."
1 Thes 5:22	"Avoid every kind of evil."
Consequences of Sexual Immorality	
2 Sam 11:2 – 18:33	The text tells about David's adultery and its results.
Psa 32:3-5	David was depressed after he committed adultery, and before he confessed his sin.
Prov 9:13-18	Adultery gives invitations to the foolish. Stolen water is sweet, but the consequences are self-destruction.

1 Cor 6:9-11	Adulterers will not inherit the Kingdom of God (9). However, God forgives the sin of adultery and frees the guilty from it (11).
Eph 5:3-17	No immoral person has any inheritance in the Kingdom of Christ (5). Live as children of light (8).
1 Cor 3:16-17	You yourselves are God's Temple; God's Spirit lives in you. God will destroy anyone who destroys his Temple.
Recover From Sexual Immorality	
2 Sam 11:2 – 12:14; Psa 32; 38; 51	After David confessed his sin of adultery, he was forgiven and again received the joy of his salvation; however, as the results of his sin, he suffered tragic consequences in his family and nation.
Hosea	The book of Hosea tells the story of a prophet who forgave his adulterous spouse.
Lk 7:36-50	A sinful woman anointed Jesus with perfume (36-39). Jesus told a parable about a debtor who loved much because he had been forgiven much (40-47). Jesus forgave the woman her sins (47-48) and said her faith had saved her (50).
Jn 4:1-26	Jesus offered "Living Water" to the Samaritan woman who had been married five times, and at that time was living with a man to whom she was not married.
1 Cor 6:9-11	Adulterers will not inherit the Kingdom of God (9). However, God forgives the sin of adultery and frees the guilty from it (11).

Sexual Immorality is related to: Addictions, Habits That Enslave a Person, Adultery and the Pastor, Change to Overcome Sin, Homosexually, Lust, Marriage, Masturbation, Marriage Sex, and Temptation.

SICKNESS

Reasons For Sickness

Lev 26:15-16	Sickness is one of the punishments for disobeying God.
Job 2:6-7	Satan inflicted Job with sickness, trying to turn him away from God.
Psa 32:3-4; 38:3-10	David experienced pain, loss of strength and depression when he was keeping silent about his sins.
Psa 107:17-18	"Some became fools through their rebellious ways and suffered affliction because of their iniquities. They loathed all food and drew near the gates of death."
Mic 6:13	Sickness may be sent as a judgment for sin.
Jn 9:1-3	The disciples thought that a certain man was born blind as a consequence of either his or his parent's sin. Jesus said that his blindness happened so that the work of God might be displayed in his life.
Jn 11:4	Jesus said that Lazarus was sick in order for God to be glorified through it.

Righteous People Suffer From Sickness

2 Ki 20:1	King Hezekiah, who faithfully served the Lord, became ill and was at the point of death.
Job 1:8; 2:7	Job was an upright man (1:8). Satan afflicted Job with painful sores (2:7).
Dan 8:27	The prophet Daniel was exhausted and lay ill for several days.
Jn 11:1-4	Jesus' friend Lazarus was sick.
Ac 9:36-37	Dorcas, who was always doing good and helping the poor, became sick and died.
Php 2:25-27	Epaphroditus, who was taking care of Paul's needs in prison, became sick and almost died.

God's Power Over Sickness

Job 2:6-7	God limited the extent to which Satan could inflict Job with sickness.

Isa 53:5	"But he (*Jesus*) was pierced for our transgressions...and by his wounds we are healed."
Psa 41:3	The righteous person is sustained by the Lord on his sickbed. It is the Lord who restores the righteous from his sickbed.
Lk 13:10-16	A woman was crippled by an evil spirit. Jesus set her free from her infirmity.
How to Deal With Sickness	
Mat 25:36, 45	Actions done in favor of the sick are considered by Jesus as actions done to him.
2 Cor 12:7-9	Paul's thorn in the flesh was a sickness given by Satan to torment him. God did not heal Paul, but gave him the grace to face it. God's power was made perfect in Paul's weakness.
Jam 5:14-16	How the church should deal with a sick member: The sick person should notify the church leaders. They should visit him and pray over him. He should be given medicine (*oil was used for medicine*) in the name of the Lord. (*The sick person's hope is not that the medicine will heal him; his hope is that the Lord will work through the medicine.*) Both the sick person and those praying for him should confess their sins. The prayers of those made righteous by confessing their sins have power and are effective.

SILENT TREATMENT

Eph 4:25	"Put off falsehood and speak truthfully." (*This is a command to speak.*)
Eph 4:26	When angry, do not sin. Resolve anger on a daily basis.
Eph 4:27	"Do not give the devil a foothold."
Eph 4:31-32	Get rid of bitterness, rage and anger.
Eph 4:32	Forgive as Christ God forgave you.
1 Cor 7:3-5	In marriage, the silent-treatment increases sexual temptations. It deprives the marriage partner of his rights. Satan's opportunity to tempt both spouses is increased; the self-control of each is diminished.

Silent treatment is related to attitude problems of: Self-Pity, Commiseration, Selfishness, Anger, Rage, Lack of Forgiveness, and the Desire for Revenge.

Silent treatment is passive aggression. It is dirty fighting; no matter what reaction the recipient of the silent treatment makes, he/she is considered wrong and the one giving the silent treatment is considered innocent.

Silent treatment closes the door to reconciliation and provokes anger. The recipient of the silent treatment is provoked to anger and desperation.

TEMPTATION

Danger of Temptation

1 Cor 9:27	Paul felt that it was necessary for him to control his body. He was afraid that after he preaches to others, he could become disqualified to receive the prize from God.
1 Cor 10:12	Danger of thinking you are standing firm.
Eph 6:12-13	Our struggle is against evil spiritual powers (12).

God's Provisions For the Person Being Tempted

Job 1:12	God limits Satan's ability to attack people.
1 Cor 1:9; 1 Tes 5:24	God is faithful.
1 Cor 10:12-13	Each temptation is common to people. God is faithful to limit temptation to one's ability to bear it, and he provides a way out.
Heb 2:18	Because Jesus was tempted, he is able to help those who are being tempted.
2 Pet 2:9	God knows how to rescue godly people from trials.
Jam 1:2-3	The testing of one's faith develops perseverance.
Jam 1:12-15	God does not tempt anyone (13). Each one is tempted by his own evil desire (14).
1 Jn 4:3-4	Victory is certain over the spirit of the antichrist. The believer in Jesus is from God, the one in the believer is greater than the one who is in the world.
1 Jn 5:4-5	Everyone born of God overcomes the world. Faith is the victory that has overcome the world.
Rev 3:10	God promised the church in Philadelphia that since they had kept his command, he would keep them from the hour of trial.

Responsibility of the One Being Tempted

Mat 6:13	Pray, asking for protection from temptation.
Eph 6:12-18	Put on the full armor of God so you can take your stand against the devil's schemes (12-13). Stand firm (14). Take up the shield of faith (16). Take the helmet of salvation and the sword of the Spirit. Pray (18). Be alert (18).

Jam 1:12-15	Persevere under trial in order to be blessed (12). Each one is tempted by his own evil desire (14).
Jam 4:7	"Submit to God. Resist the devil, and he will flee from you."
1 Jn 5:4-5	Have faith. Faith is the victory that has overcome the world.

THANKFULNESS TO GOD

Deut 8:7-10	"For the Lord your God is bringing you into a good land....When you have eaten and are satisfied, praise the Lord your God for the good land he has given you."
Psa 69:30	"I will praise God's name in song and glorify him with thanksgiving. This will please the Lord."
Psa 95:2	"Let us come before him (*God*) with thanksgiving."
Psa 105:1	"Give thanks to the Lord."
Eph 5:20	"Always giving thanks to God the Father for everything, in the name of our Lord Jesus Christ."
Php 4:6	Instead of worrying, pray, making your petition with thanksgiving.
Col 2:6-7	Continue to live in Christ, overflowing with thankfulness.
Col 3:15-17	Let the peace of Christ rule in your hearts. Be thankful.
1 Thes 5:18	"Give thanks in all circumstances, for this is God's will for you in Christ Jesus."
1 Tim 2:1	Requests, prayers, intercession and thanksgiving should be made for everyone.
Examples of Thankfulness	
Psa 68:19; 119:62	The psalmist praised the Lord.
Dan 2:23	Daniel gave thanks to God for answered prayer, "I thank and praise you, O God of my fathers: You have given me wisdom and power, you have made known to me what we asked of you, you have made known to us the dream of the king."
Mat 11:25	Jesus gave thanks for the things that God had revealed to the "little people."
Jn 6:8-11	Jesus took five small barley loaves and two small fish, gave thanks and distributed the bread and fish to a multitude of about 5,000 men.
Jn 11:41	Before raising Lazarus from the dead, Jesus gave thanks that the Father had heard him.

Ac 28:15	Paul gave thanks to God when some brothers met him on his journey to Rome.
1 Cor 15:57	Paul said, "But thanks be to God! He gives us the victory through our Lord Jesus Christ."
Php 1:3	Every time Paul remembered the Philippians, he gave thanks to God.
Col 1:3-4	Paul always thanked God when he prayed for the problematic Colossians.
1 Thes 1:2	Paul gave thanks to God for the Thessalonians, mentioning them in his prayers.
Examples of Lack of Thankfulness	
Lk 17:17-18	Nine of the ten who were healed of leprosy did not return to give thanks to Jesus.
Rom 1:21	Ingratitude is a characteristic of the ungodly.

TOXIC PARENTS

Ex 20:12; Eph 6:1-2	The Bible commands children to honor their parents.
1 Kg 15:9-14	King Asa was faithful to the Lord. His own grandmother Maacah had made a idol to Asheral. Asa burned the idol and removed Maacah form her position as queen mother.
Prov 4:27	Walk away; remove your feet from evil. *(This could permit the adult child of evil parents to walk away from them.)*
Jer 29:11	God plans for his people to have peace and not disaster, and a future filled with hope. *(Abuse from a parent is not God's plan for his people.)*
Mat 5:43-45	Jesus taught his disciples to pray for those who persecute them. *(Those who are persecuted by toxic parents have the duty to pray for them.)*
Mat 6:14-15; Jam 2:13	Forgive those who have done you wrong, just like you want God to forgive you. Refuse to forgive others and God will refuse to forgive you.
Mat 10:34-39	Christ came to bring division. *(Following Christ may require an adult child to separate from his toxic parent in order to put an end to an abusive relationship.)*
Mat 18:6	Jesus taught that a person who causes a child to sin would be better off if he drowned in the sea with a large stone hung around his neck. *(Jesus placed the toxic parent who caused their children to sin under a curse. He would not expect those children to give honor to those whom he places under a curse.)*
Rom 16:17	Watch out and stay away from people who cause divisions and make others fall away from the Christian faith.
1 Cor 15:33	Associating with bad people will corrupt the person with good character. *(Evil parents can corrupt their own children.)*
Eph 6:4	Parents are not to make their children bitter about life. *(Parents who abuse their children are in the wrong.)*

Rom 12:18	As much as depends on you, live at peace with everyone. *(Try to have peace with toxic parents but recognize that some parents will never have peace with their children.)*

"Toxic parent" describes the parent whose own negative behavior inflicts physical, emotional, or spiritual damage to their children. A difference exists between imperfect parents who made mistakes, and evil toxic parents who abuse their children or failed to protect them.

People who are cruel, addicts, angry, abusive, pedophiles, narcissistic, irresponsible, manipulative, or mentally ill can have sex and as a result become parents.

The Bible says to honor your parents, but it doesn't address what to do when they are dishonoring themselves. God tells us to stay away from evil and to rebuke evil. Toxic parents do not have an exemption from this rule. God would not contradict himself by saying rebuke evil at one time and honor it at another.

Toxic parents create situations that cannot be changed. The best way to handle things that cannot be changed is to practice accepting the way things are and deciding to get on with life in spite of the situation. Acceptance is reaching the conclusion:
- This is how my toxic parents are.
- It's not how God meant them to be.
- It's not how I want them to be.
- I accept that this is how they are.
- I will get on with my life doing what God wants me to do and becoming who God wants me to be.

Ways to honor toxic parents:
- Don't return the abuse that they give you.
- Don't try to destroy their lives; seek to transform them through Christ.
- Pray for their salvation and for their break though from toxic behavior.
- Stop trying to save or change them yourself, that is Christ's job.
- Don't do things that help enable them to continue their abuses or addictions.
- Establish clear boundaries and consequences.
- Reverse the curse of a dysfunctional home; don't allow their abusive legacy to continue to your children.

- Avoid putting yourself, as their child, in a position to be abused.

    Forgiveness is a tough one in regards to toxic parents.
- Forgiveness lets go of the feeling that your toxic parent owes you a debt and you have the duty to make him pay.
- Forgiveness lets go of anger and resentment.
- When a toxic parent is remorseful and changes abusive behavior, the child should be open to reconciliation. However, if a parent is not remorseful, does not change, and continues to be abusive, the child is not condemned to have an abusive, toxic relationship with an evil person who happens to be his parent.
- Forgiveness does not require reconciliation. You can't reconcile with someone who hurts you repeatedly, and won't change. Forgiving the toxic abusive parent; verses, protecting yourself through estrangement, are two entirely different things.
- Forgiveness doesn't mean excusing what someone did, or justifying it, or pretending it never happened.
- Christ laid his life down for the toxic, evil, rebellious people who hated him. People who put their trust in Christ will be given the grace to forgive their toxic parent who hurt them.

VIOLENCE

Gen 6:13	One of the reasons God gave for destroying the world with the flood was the fact that people had filled the earth with violence.
Psa 73:6	Violence is a characteristic of the wicked (6). They obtain prosperity through violence (3).
Prov 4:17	Violence is a characteristic of the wicked.
Isa 2:4	Violence will cease in the Messianic Age when men shall beat their swords into plows.
Isa 59:2, 6	Violence is included in the list of sins which separates people from God and prevents him from hearing their prayers.
Jer 6:6-7	Violence calls for God's punishment.
Eze 8:17-18	Violence provokes God to anger (17) and prevents him from hearing prayers (18).
Am 3:10	The violent person does not know how to do right.
Mic 2:2	The powerful, who use violence, will suffer God's punishment.
Mic 6:12	The injustice and violence of the rich are condemned.
Mat 11:12	The Kingdom of God suffers attacks from violent people.
Lk 3:14	Don't use violence to extort money.

Violence is a result of sin and rebellion against God.

Observation:

There are occasions when love, which seeks the well-being of others, may require violence.
Examples:
- It may become necessary to hit a panicked person drowning in a lake in order to save their life.
- If one happens upon an aggressor who is hurting an innocent or defenseless person, violence may become necessary in order to defend and protect the victim.

WORK

Gen 2:5, 15	After the creation, man was to work and care for the Garden of Eden.
Gen 3:17-19	After Adam and Eve sinned, work became painful toil and was often unproductive.
Prov 12:11	"He who works his land will have abundant food; he who chases fantasies lacks judgment."
Prov 14:23	Hard work brings a profit.
Prov 18:9	"One who is slack in his work is brother to one who destroys."
Prov 21:5	The plans of the diligent lead to profit.
Prov 22:29	A skilled worker will be promoted and recognized.
Prov 24:27	Take care of business and make preparations for food before starting a family.
Prov 31:10-31	The wife of noble character is a hard worker.
Ecc 5:12	"The sleep of a laborer is sweet, whether he eats little or much."
1 Cor 15:58	Give yourselves fully to the work of the Lord. Your labor in the Lord is not in vain.
Eph 4:28	The thief must stop stealing and start working. He must start sharing with the needy.
Col 3:22-24	Work at whatever you do with all your heart.
1 Thes 4:11	"Make it your ambition to lead a quiet life, to mind your own business and to work with your hands."
2 Thes 3:6-15	Keep away from the person who refuses to work (6). Paul was an example of one who worked hard (7-9). Do not feed a person who refuses to work (10).

	WORRY
Psa 37:1-8	"Do not fret because of evil men" (1). "Trust in the Lord and do good" (3). "Delight yourself in the Lord" (4). "Commit your way to the Lord" (5). "Be still before the Lord and wait patiently for him" (7). "Do not fret; it leads only to evil" (8).
Psa 127:2	"In vain you rise early and stay up late, toiling for food to eat – for he (God) grants sleep to those he loves."
Prov 12:25	An anxious heart weighs a person down.
Prov 17:22	"A cheerful heart is good medicine, but a crushed spirit dries up the bones."
Mat 6:25-34	Do not worry about your life (25), about food (25), or about clothes (28). Worry is an attitude common to pagans. Worry is unnecessary because we have a Father in Heaven (32). Solution to worry: Seek first God's Kingdom. Do not worry about tomorrow; live today (34).
Mat 13:7, 22	In the Parable of the Sower, Jesus explained that the worries of this life will choke the Word of God.
Lk 10:38-41	Martha's worry about many things kept her from giving attention to the most important thing.
Lk 12:11	Jesus forbade his disciples to have anxiety when facing persecution for his sake.
Php 4:6-7	Do not be anxious; instead, pray with petitions and thanksgiving. Then the peace of God will guard your hearts and minds in Christ Jesus.
1 Pet 5:6-7	God's mighty hand is able to lift you up. Cast your anxiety on him because he cares for you. *(A person has a choice: turn his worry over to God or hold on to it by himself.)*

Worry is related to: Fear.

PLAN FOR DEALING WITH LIFE-ISSUES

The Christian leader should determine by the grace of God to know and use the Scripture in dealing with life-issues. He should use the Scripture to deal with his own life-issues as well as to help those who look to him for guidance.

The use of Scripture in dealing with life-issues involves the following factors:

1. **An understanding of the life-issue you are dealing with**
   Discover the details of what happened and the reactions of each person involved.

2. **A biblical understanding of the life-issues involved**
   Discover what the Scripture has to say about the life-issue, and about the different reactions of each person involved.
   It is important to know what God intended to do with the Scripture that speaks about the life-issue (command, warn, encourage, motivate, condemn, etc.). The text should be used for the same purpose as God first intended.

3. **A bringing together of the life-issue with biblical teaching**
   There needs to be a meeting of today's life-issues with God's solution as found in the Scripture. Make notes on what the Bible has to say about the life-issue being dealt with and about each reaction of each person involved. Give special attention to finding biblical commands and promises that relate to both the life-issue and to each reaction. Then find biblical stories of people who faced similar life-issues or who had similar reactions to other life-issues.

4. **A formulation of a biblical plan of action that deals with the life-issue and with actions and reactions of those involved**
   Formulate a plan to deal with the issue and to resolve other issues which developed as a result of reactions to the issue. The plan should follow biblical principles to work through the life-issue.
   A biblical plan of action: (1) is based on biblical teaching and Scripture, (2) aims to achieve biblical goals; (3) follows biblical methods and (4) is pursued from biblical motives.

I advise people to write out specific concrete plans of action for dealing with their life-issues. Two people dealing with a similar issue may come up with completely different action plans. That is to be expected. However, it is essential that each person's plans for action agree with biblical teachings and principles.

5. **A commitment of all involved to obey biblical teachings and to follow biblical principles in dealing with the life-issue**

    Challenge each person involved to commit themselves to obey biblical teachings and to follow biblical principles in dealing with the life issue.

I have found that the table on the following page helps me deal with my own life-issues. I use it when I am helping others deal with their life-issues.

PLAN FOR DEALING WITH LIFE-ISSUES

THE ISSUE	YOUR REACTION	BIBLICAL REACTIONS	BIBLICAL RESPONSE
What happened	Emotions, thoughts, actions, reactions, reactions to another person's actions etc.	Biblical references related to both the problem and reactions. Include biblical commands and promises, and stories of Bible characters who faced similar issues.	Specific action plans based on biblical principles to deal with the life-issue and to correct improper reactions.